A GOO

Rita F. Snowden is widel[...] the author of more than [...] dren. After six years at bu[...] she trained as a deaconess of the New Zealand Methodist Church, serving in turn two pioneer country areas before moving to the largest city for several years of social work during an economic depression.

Miss Snowden has served the world Church, beyond her own denomination, with regular broadcasting commitments. She has written and spoken in Britain, Canada, the United States, in Australia, and in Tonga at the invitation of Queen Salote. She has represented her church at the World Methodist Conference in Oxford; later being elected the first woman Vice-President of the New Zealand Methodist Church, and President of its Deaconess Association. She has been an Honorary Vice-President of the New Zealand Women Writers' Society, and is a Fellow of the International Institute of Arts and Letters, and a member of P.E.N.

Miss Snowden has been honoured by the award of the Order of the British Empire, and by the citation of "The Upper Room" in America.

Her most recent books are *Prayers for Busy People, Christianity Close to Life, Bedtime Stories and Prayers* (for children), *I Believe Here and Now, Discoveries That Delight, Further Good News, Continually Aware, Good Company, Prayers in Large Print, Like Wind on the Grasses, Secrets* and *People and Places*.

Rita F. Snowden

A GOOD HARVEST

*Fresh daily thoughts
and prayers*

Collins
FOUNT PAPERBACKS

First published in Great Britain by
Fount Paperbacks, London in 1988

Made and printed in Great Britain by
William Collins Sons & Co. Ltd, Glasgow

*Unless otherwise specified, biblical quotations come from the
Authorized Version of the Bible.*

In life here, our God gives
A share of His gold sun;
For sad sleep, new mornings;
Hard work, much lively fun;
For strained muscles, sweet rest;
Above dullness, a song;
To waiting fields – HARVEST!

R.F.S.

CONTENTS

Introduction

In the gracious countryside where I grew up, Harvest was widespread – and very joyous! It earned an early place in my autobiography, *The Sun is High*. But since that book is no longer available, I will digest a few paragraphs to spell out *the spirit of Harvest*!

The seasons moved like a backcloth to familiar characters. We children were born and lived in "Clover Road" – though it was a long time before we knew it had a name. It was just "our road", meandering down from the hills, from beyond which each new day came to us, losing itself in the grass at the riverside, and its loved trees. Sometimes, a "swagger" would come our way, with a hunger and thirst, but otherwise we knew all who travelled up and down, and what business they had. One and another would greet us: "'Lo, children!" "'Lo, George!"

When the season and our father were alike ready, he guided the plough down the sweet furrow, with gulls from the sea, six miles off, following after. Seed, in time, was hopefully sown, and growth awaited, hedges were clipped. (Much water has run under the old bridge, and growth been clipped from the hedges, since I sighted my first nestful of young birds, their gaping yellow beaks opened widely to a beneficent world. All purpose then was in an hour, all Summer in a flower!)

Part of our farm was in white clover; and countless bee stings I got through the open sides of my sandals, as I crossed by a thread of path, carrying my father's tea.

And there was the orchard. We children always discovered the first green gooseberries that ripened sweet, followed by the big fat veined ones, whose delicious insides popped out rudely as we bit into them. We had free run of the orchard – save for apricots, peaches and pears which belonged to the kingdom of grown-ups. Like Eden, these knew restrictions: our mother stood over against them, as with a flaming sword, with a view to jams and preserves. (Till I was in my 'teens, a student away from home, I never bought fruit, or saw it set on a table at a meal time – to us, fruit wasn't food, if uncooked, it was just fruit.) We never lacked plums, apples, figs and nuts to bulge our pockets when we were sent to fetch the cows for milking; to gather chips from the woodblock in the yard, to start up the stove; or get the evening newspaper thrown from the guard's van of the train that passed a handy distance off. It was my routine task for years, to run that distance with my hoop, and bring the paper back. Sometimes it was carelessly thrown, as the train speeded by, to be lost in the tall grasses.

Season by season, our ears knew the hiss of the scythe, the whirr of the hone sharpening the blade; and morning by morning, a thrush singing from a neighbouring treetop:

> *Get up, get!*
> *Be quick, be quick!*
> *Stick to it, stick to it!*

When Harvest was fully come, great billies of tea had to go to the brown-armed men sweltering under the high sun. Neighbours came to help. The Sigglekow sons brought, as well as their pitchforks, their mouth organs, and in odd moments of leisure taught us to sing, "Pretty Red-wing". There, under the stack's grateful shade, we shared lunchtimes together. In comparison with the neighbouring fathers whom we knew, these lounging, laughing young men seemed like giants and minstrels from another world!

At season's end, the engine-and-thresher lumbered into our stackyard, putting in an appearance the night before

10

the work was to begin. Next morning, our mother found difficulty in keeping us at table long enough to eat our plates of porridge. Things more exciting were happening. By the time we could squeeze through the opening in the fence the engine would be merry with smoke and steam, its flywheel turning with all the importance of the universe. The little cluster of balls that our father called "the governor" – half-way along the body of the monster – winked already in the sunshine. An enormous belt swung between engine and thresher.

Two known men with pitchforks stood balanced against the sky, high up, waiting to fill the yammering innards of the thresher. By late afternoon, we knew they would be brought down from their exalted position. But we envied them. At the end of the long elevator, soon only distracted straw would come down to earth, spewed out golden. There two other men stood, set on building a new stack – but to us, never to hold the prestige of the first: it wasn't built by our father; and it was only made of straw.

Yet another stranger attended to that part of the thresher's anatomy where grain appeared. We couldn't help wondering what would happen if he, for a moment, forgot to hook on the empty sack. We waited, but that crisis never occurred. When each sack was full, he deftly shut off the supply, swung the sack onto a set of iron scales, and, threading his gleaming needle with astonishing speed, just as quickly sewed up the sack.

Always to our sorrow, the time came when the engine-and-thresher were suddenly gone, and all belonging to them. Only full sacks of corn remained, as did the strawstack, large and oblong. It was slippery at first, and smelled nice. But its freshness passed soon, and it settled down, to be burrowed into by children, calves, and cows. Early evening – with the heat of the day exchanged for the cool of oncoming night, the big moths flying, the moon

11

golden, round, and high over the hills – was all part of Harvest.

Then a home window would show a soft light, and we would be called indoors – glad at heart to drag off our boots, stockings and clothes, wash, and then clamber into bed. Harvest was that kind of rich experience. A memory that cannot be effaced!

* * *

And Harvest, in an even deeper, richer sense, is meaningful to me! My ongoing Faith sends me continually to a striking verse in The New English Bible: **The Harvest of the Spirit** is Love, Joy, Peace, Patience, Kindness, Goodness, Fidelity, Gentleness, and Self-control" (Galatians 5:22). Nine choice values! Nine lasting realities! Certainly "*A Good Harvest*"!

And here I am, taking pleasure in sharing a little of what I have gathered of each of them, one by one, till now. In a slight book like this, it is not, of course, possible to cover them all fully. In any case, they belong to an ever-enlarged experience!

But I hope that what I have written will be of worth to you. Each section will start with an essential space – for Silence. I work on the assumption that all of us live busy lives, day by day, very likely not doing the same things, *but many things*!

And our ages make a difference, too!

It's not only the beloved Mother Teresa, amongst us living today, who says, as she does: "*God is the Friend of Silence*! See how Nature – trees, flowers, grass – grow in silence: see the stars, the moon and sun, how they move in silence . . . The more we receive in silent prayer, the more we can give in our active life . . . Words can so often increase the darkness."

Doctor Johnson, wise old spirit, is remembered to have

said: "A man should keep his friendships in constant repair." No one of us doubts that, man or woman. And something very like it, is part of our richer relationship with God – **speaking** and **listening**! The Psalmist, early on, was clear on these two essentials. His words were: "*Hear me* speedily, O Lord . . . *Cause me to hear*" (Psalm 143, verses 7 & 8). That's the abiding structure of Prayer: it's a close relationship with God; a fellowship with the Father of our Lord Christ, *our* eternal, Living, Loving Creator. Of course, it's not only asking for things; it's also seeking to establish a close awareness; a deep desire, here and now, to lead one's faltering, creaturely will, to the Will of our Gracious Everlasting God, through Christ. So the spirit of one's approach is *not* "do for me what I want"; but "*do with me* what *You will*"!

And one isn't required to use any particular words, much less high-sounding phrases from holy occasions of long ago. Prayer is as natural as anything else that has a daily place in our lives, and it is counted as precious as our very breath. Someone has described it, in stumbling words, as "Like lifting up one's eyes to the hills, and knowing their strength, and one's own littleness. At other times, like going into a place so clean, that one draws back, lest he or she soil that cleanness. Or it's like standing in one's open doorway, once more full of warmth, after a long time of being a stranger in a strange land. It is like receiving a gift beyond all expectation, and not knowing what to say that seems fitting. It's like all these – but it's not the same as any of them."

Another fell back on one of the world's greatest stories, that of a youth who ran off, wild-headed, into a far country – and one day came back to find his Loving Father, with eyes long shaded against the light, picking out a tiny distant whirl of dust raised by the feet of one he missed terribly. *Prayer*, one discovers, *is an essential part of knowing that one belongs to the Divine Father*. (If one could know it only once in a lifetime, how wonderful it would be! But prayer spells out this merciful relationship constantly, and wherever one chances to be.)

"The energy of Love", using Dr C.H. Dodd's words, sharing this rich discovery, "discharges itself along the lines which form a triangle whose points are God, self, and neighbour." And without that Divine gift, earth knowledge has an academic and clinical chill.

> *Love ever gives –*
> *Forgives – outlives –*
> *And ever stands*
> *With open hands*
>
> *And while it lives*
> *It gives –*
> *For this is Love's prerogative!*
> *To give and give and give.*

"*God is Love; and he that dwelleth in Love dwelleth in God, and God in him*" (1 John 4:16; The Epistle).

*

Unless otherwise specified, the prayers in this book are by the author.

LOVE

The Harvest of the Spirit is Love

In life here, most of us find Love a strong, glorious thing. But on the street, often what we see, overhear, and happen on – as readers of newspapers, and scanners of novels and magazines – is otherwise. There are even times when we are nauseated by what films, radio, and T.V. bring us.

It's not often, when reading a modern book of poems, we are asked to give thanks that "Because of your strong love I held my path". At sight of such a dedication, one's heart lifts up! And it was with surprise that I learned of Bertrand Russell, the distinguished philosopher, who, among other public addresses, gave one on "Why I am *not* a Christian" but, later, asked on his eightieth birthday what it was he felt that "the world stood most in need of", answered: "The root of the matter is a very simple, and old-fashioned thing, a thing so simple that I am almost ashamed to mention it, for fear of the derisive smile with which wise cynics will greet my words. The thing – please forgive me for mentioning it – is *Love, Christian Love*."

And he then felt he wanted to add: "If you feel this, you have a motive for existence, a reason for courage, an imperative necessity for intellectual honesty."

And this kind of Love, we discover as we go along, is known to many ordinary men and women here and now, in uncommonly fine home-making, and family life. It is more than a fleeting emotional experience, a mixture of passion and sentimentality, wrapped in glamour on rare occasions, accompanied with a bouquet, and flowery buttonhole.

Something very different, recognizable by most of us, shines out through Elizabeth Barrett Browning's poem to

17

her husband, Robert. For all that they were both poets, it is gloriously close to life:

> How do I love thee? *Let me count the ways*.
> I love thee to the depth and breadth and height
> My soul can reach when feeling out of sight
> For the ends of Being and ideal Grace.
> I love thee to the level of every day's
> Most quiet need, by sun and candle-light,
> I love thee freely, as men strive for Right;
> I love thee purely, as they turn from Praise.
> I love thee with the passion put to use
> In my old griefs, and with my childhood's faith.
> I love thee with a love I seemed to lose
> With my lost saints – I love thee with the breath,
> Smiles, tears, of all my life! – and if God choose,
> I shall but love thee better after Death.

But we must recognize these great qualities, in measure, *also beyond marriage*. For some people are dedicated to the Church, the Arts, a missionary life overseas, or a healing ministry – as was Florence Allshorn, the gracious, practical, endlessly self-giving founder of "St Julian's", a retreat and Christian adventure house, set in the English countryside of our day. (Dr J.H. Oldham wrote her life-story, telling of her work both overseas and at St Julian's, which was published by the SCM Press in 1951.) And as long as there are men and women among us concerned with the primary values of Love, her own books ought never to go out of print. Therein lies something for us all, right out of a glad, gay, dedicated spirit: "I am so troubled", she once wrote, "*about not loving people enough.*"

"I used to think", she wrote, "that there was something in me too precious to run the risk of mixing with ugly, ordinary things – a kind of mystical dream of something that might grow into something very beautiful, if I kept my mind up in the clouds enough and did not allow it to be soiled. I can't explain it, but it was purely selfish. And now I know that life is clean, dirty, ugly, beautiful, wonderful, sordid – *and above all, Love.*"

And as her experience deepened and widened, she added: "To love a human being means to accept him, *to love him as he is*. If you wait to love him till he has got rid of his faults, till he is different, you are only loving an idea. He is as he is now, and he is to be loved now, as he is . . . To love him with the love of Christ means first of all to accept him as he is, and then try and lead him towards a goal he doesn't see yet – and because I love, to attack all that is contrary to God with all the energy of Love.

"Christ's Love is exactly like that; it is entirely disinterested and self-less; it accepts you as you are, with all that is displeasing and even painful for Him, in you; it gives Love whatever the response may be; it forgives and forgives endlessly."

This, one has to learn, is the nature of Love – set, to this day, *foremost* in **The Harvest of the Spirit**!

* * *

Says Peter Stephens, in our day:

"God loves in a way that surpasses human love. We love *some people and not others*. We love people *some of the time*, but not all of the time. We love people *while it pays*, and we stop when it doesn't.

"*But God's love isn't patchy.* It isn't for some people, for some of the time. It is for all . . . for all the time. He loves not only the good, but the evil. He enters our human situation, is born, lives, suffers, and dies to win men into a new way of life, a life of love and trust. (The New Testament is quite clear: 'God did not send His Son into the world to condemn the world; but that the world through Him might be saved' (John 3:17.)

"As we look at the life of Christ", adds Peter Stephens, "(and that is the best picture we have of God) we see One whose whole life was spent in reaching out to men *in love*. To religious and irreligious, to moral and immoral, to Pharisee and to publican He went, seeking to put them *on a new footing with God*.

"Man's will means man's freedom to accept or reject God's will. When you say, '*Why doesn't God make man believe*?' then you are demanding that men become mere puppets. But if they did, they would cease to be men. If men are to be men, they must have freedom – freedom to choose, freedom to accept or reject."

* * *

Choice lies at the very heart of Love – God's Love, and every expression of human love, as we are allowed to experience it here. Horatius Bonar, the loved hymn-writer, gloried in this, in a hymn he gave our world a century back, and which we sing still:

O Love of God, how strong and true;
Eternal, and yet ever new;
Uncomprehended and unbought,
Beyond all knowledge and all thought!

O heavenly Love, how precious still,
In days of weariness and ill,
In nights of pain and helplessness,
To heal, to comfort, and to bless.

O wide-embracing, wondrous Love;
We read Thee in the sky above,
We read Thee in the earth below,
In seas that swell and streams that flow.

We read thee best in Him who came
To bear for us the Cross of shame,
Sent by the Father from on high,
Our life to live, our death to die.

*

Another sings:
My song is Love . . .
my Saviour's Love to me,
love to the loveless shown,
that they might lovely be.
O who am I
that for my sake
my Lord should take
frail flesh, and die?

He came from his blest throne
salvation to bestow;
but men made strange, and none
the longed-for Christ would know,
But O my friend!
my friend, indeed,
who at my need
His life did spend.

Sometimes they strew His way
and His sweet praises sing,
resounding all the day
hosannas to their King.
Then "Crucify!"
is all their breath
and for His death
they thirst and cry.   (*Samuel Grossman, 1624-84*)

We can only humbly bow our heads in His presence, and confess our own shortcomings. "I am so troubled *about*

not loving people enough", as Florence Allshorn con-
fessed.

For a whole year she read the thirteenth chapter of the
First Epistle to the Corinthians, *every day*. And the words
with which Paul finished it, were as the words of the Lord
to her: "**Make Love your aim**!" (Might this not be a lasting
help to you? To me?)

Prayers

Prayers to mingle with my own

O Master Christ,
Thou hast loved us with an everlasting Love:
Thou hast forgiven us, trained us, disciplined us;
Thou hast broken us loose and laid Thy commands
    upon us;
Thou hast set us in the thick of things, and deigned
    to use us;
Thou hast shown thyself to us, fed us, guided us;
Be graciously pleased to accept and forgive our poor
    efforts.
And keep us Thy free bondslaves for ever.
(Writer unknown, but offered in *A Diary of Prayer*
    by Elizabeth Goudge, Hodder and Stoughton)

Praise For All Seasons

When Spring comes laughing
    By vale and hill,
By wind-flower walking
    And daffodil –

Sing stars of morning,
  Sing morning skies,
Sing blue of speedwell –
  And my Love's eyes.

When comes the Summer,
  Full-leaved and strong,
And gay birds gossip
The orchard long –
  Sing bird, sweet honey
That no bee sips;
Sing red, red roses –
  And my love's lips.

When Autumn scatters
  The leaves again
And piled sheaves bury
  The broad-wheeled wain –
Sing flutes of harvest
  Where men rejoice;
Sing rounds of reapers –
  And my Love's voice.

But when comes Winter
  With hail and storm,
And red fire roaring,
  And ingle warm,
Sing first sad going
  Of friends that part;
Then sing glad meeting –
  And my Love's heart.   (*Austin Dobson*)

Prayer on Waking

Awake, my Soul, and with the sun
Thy daily stage of duty run;

Shake off dull sloth, and joyful rise
To pay thy morning sacrifice.

Glory to Thee, who safe hast kept
And hast refresh'd me whilst I slept;
Grant, Lord, when I from death shall wake,
I may of endless light partake.

Lord, I my vows to Thee renew;
Scatter my sins as morning dew;
Guard my first springs of thought and will,
And with Thyself my spirit fill.

Direct, control, suggest, *this day*,
All I design, or do, or say;
That all my powers, with all their might,
In Thy sole glory may unite.

(Bishop Thomas Ken)

Grant, O Lord, that none may love
Thee less this day because of me.
That never word or act of mine
May turn one soul from Thee.
And, ever daring, yet one other
grace would I implore –
That many souls this day, because
of me, may love Thee more.

(Medieval Prayer)

To his friends in the early church, Paul wrote from his heart:

Let your Love be a real thing.

(Now in Romans 12:9; Moffatt translation)

Prayers

For The Morning

Ever gracious God, I waken to the delights and difficulties of a new day, thankful for safe-keeping through the night. It is wonderful to know that this great world spinning in space, is Yours – and that I, too, am Yours.

Save me from thinking of myself this day as of little importance – and conversely, as of too great importance, as I move amongst people. Many will have claims upon me, as this day opens out. Let the Faith which is mine prove sufficient for the needs of this day.

Quicken, I pray, my capacity to love You this day; and to love all with whom I share its ongoing hours.

I rejoice in the good gift of life, which comes from You continually; the warmth of the sun; and the cheerful colours of grass and gardens. I rejoice in the trustfulness of many animals; I rejoice in birds with neat plumage, and cheerful songs. I give thanks for great trees, with heads high against the skies, and for their welcome shade, for their usefulness in our human life.

For the mountains, and for supporting hills up-raised, I bless You. For the loveliness of lakes and streams; and for rivers finding their way to boundless seas. For beaches, and for the beauty, relaxation and fun they bring – for deep seas that link country with country, and islands with islands.

Help us to use well, this day, our precious energies – our particular skills learned through the years, and all natural gifts and graces.

And where I cannot sincerely offer Love today, let me at least show respect, I pray. In the Spirit of Christ, AMEN.

For the Evening

Merciful Father, You have blessed me this day, in my "going out"; bless me now, in my "coming in". From time beyond remembrance, men and women have hushed their hearts to pray at day's end – and I do that now.

Here, in this loved and familiar place, shedding all pretence, I beg Your ever-ready forgiveness, where I have acted foolishly today, or embraced ideas or relationships unworthy of my discipleship. I humbly bow my head before You – in words spoken – and also in reverent silence.

I commit now to Your keeping, all those dear to me, near and far, young and old, each with cause for special thanksgiving, this night. The needs of some *only* are known to me – but I greatly rejoice that *all* are known to You. I name ———————— especially; and ———————— and ———————— in Your presence. Yet they can never be anywhere else. Hold us all, in Your mighty, supportive Love this night. In Christ's Name. AMEN.

JOY

The Harvest of the Spirit is Joy

Many artists, even some notable ones, from medieval times down to this day, have done humanity a disservice in that they have shown us Jesus with a sad face, as "The Man of Sorrows", a name He rightly bears – but never as "*The Man of Joy*".

Somehow, they have overlooked the glorious fact that the word "Joy", along with "great joy", appears no less than *fifty-three times* in our New Testament. And to miss this is an irreparable loss. Clearly, the New Testament is a joyous book! And if the corners of our mouths are continually down, something is amiss with our Christianity. (We're not talking here of "jollity", we're talking of Joy, and there's a great difference: the first can be a momentary, slight thing. But Joy has deep roots.) For all that, it is not possible to command it in another: "Come, show us some Joy!"

At Bethlehem it was present, at the world's first Christmas – with the singing of angels, and the steps of simple shepherds instantly responding with the words: "Let us go now even unto Bethlehem, and see this thing which is come to pass!" (Luke 2:15). To the world, this was the Birth of Jesus, to be "The Man of Joy"!

And it was no ordinary Joy – at the mercy of things that could happen. Not at all! Even, years on, when the shadow of the Cross began to appear, He said to His close disciples in the Upper Room: "These things have I spoken unto You that *My Joy may be in you, and that your Joy may be fulfilled*" (John 15:11). And again: "Ye therefore now have sorrow; but I will see you again . . . *and your Joy no one taketh away from you*" (John 16:22). (And it

29

was so – even beyond the agony and shame of the Crucifixion, came the Joy of the Resurrection, followed by what may have seemed likely to be a sad parting. But no: the reality of His physical parting and ascension was otherwise.) The New Testament says of those same disciples and their friends: "They returned to Jerusalem *with great Joy*." (Luke 24:52). They weren't a tearful, distressed funeral party, returning home, with all the good and gracious times of fellowship at an end. Not at all. They had exchanged His physical presence, for His spiritual Presence, *alive for ever more*!

Barnabas was soon to call those followers of the Risen, Ascended Christ, *"The children of Joy"*!

A number of His disciples had seen that ministry begin; in little Cana of Galilee (John 2:1). Jesus had been invited to a wedding of joy – not because He was a pious person who could be counted on to speak "a good word in season", but because *He was a supremely Joyous Person*!

I recalled that myself in one of our city churches. I was attending a great conference of ministers, deaconesses and laity. And I found myself unexpectedly sitting beside an organist friend, Addie. Soon, next to me on the other side, appeared a small boy – a very small boy – with a piece of chewing gum. He was pulling it in and out, making fantastic patterns with it. There was no other child anywhere in that august company. Soon, the little fellow whispered: "Isn't the organ going to play?" "No, no, not today", I was obliged to answer. "Then, I'd better be going", he whispered, and with that, slipped out.

Later, when we came out of conference, my friend said to me: "I'm sure that little fellow was one of three who came here in the holidays. I was deputizing for the organist; and that afternoon, as I was practising, I heard children's voices. I turned on my stool, and three of them were standing just inside the church. I called: 'You mustn't play in here; this is the church.' One of them answered: 'Oh, we came to hear the organ.' 'Well, if that is what you want, you'd better come up here, and see it as well,' I said, 'all its wonderful stops and keys.'"

"At such close range", said my friend, "they were speechless. Then, the little one of the trio – about seven – looked up beseechingly with, 'Miss, could you play "Here comes the bride"?'"

"And what did you do?" I asked. "I played it for her", said my friend, "I played it for her childish joy – 'Here comes the bride'!"

And my friend's reply pleased me – as I am sure it would please our Lord and Master, who began His public ministry at a wedding feast! (He loved little children, and shared their joy in *playing weddings* – as well as funerals – in the marketplace) (Luke 7:32).

I stuffed my conference agenda into my bag that evening with special satisfaction, and made my way home at the end of a busy day, thinking of our Lord's joy! (I remembered His words to His disciple friends toward the end of one of their days together, never to be forgotten: "*My joy I give unto you,*" He said, "*and your joy no man taketh from you*") (John 16:22).

Somewhere, in an early century, the beloved St Bernard of Clairvaux sang about it; and in church we still sing his words, challenging "sullen saints" among us:

> *Jesu, Thou Joy of loving hearts,*
> *Thou Fount of life, Thou Light of men,*
> *From the best bliss that earth imparts*
> *We turn unfilled to Thee again*!

* * *

John Bunyan, during the days when he was still in the middle of his doubts and fears and problems, tells of hearing some humble women, who were true and lively

Christians, talk of their religion. They did not know that he was listening. But he wrote of them: "*Methinks they spoke as if Joy did make them speak*." And countless others since, have prompted such remarks.

To read, and maybe memorize

Old Testament

"And all the people gathered themselves together as one man into the street that was before the water gate; and they spake unto Ezra the scribe to bring the book of the law of Moses, which the Lord had commanded to Israel. And Ezra the priest brought the law before the congregation both of men and women, and all that could hear with understanding . . . Then he said unto them, *Go your way . . . for the joy of the Lord is your strength*" (Nehemiah 8:1, 2, 10).

*

"My soul shall *be joyful in the Lord*: it shall rejoice in His salvation." (Psalm 35:9).

New Testament

Said Jesus: "If ye keep My commandments, ye shall abide in My love; even as I have kept My Father's commandments, and abide in His love.

"These things have I spoken unto you, *that My Joy might remain in you, and that your Joy might be full*." (Words to His disciples, recorded in John 15:10, 11).

*

As for Saul, he made havoc of the church, entering into

every house, and haling men and women committed them to prison.

Therefore they that were scattered abroad went everywhere preaching the Word.

Then Philip went down to the city of Samaria, and preached Christ unto them. And the people with one accord gave heed unto those things which Philip spake, hearing and seeing the miracles which he did . . . *And there was great Joy in that city*. (Part of the early, costly witness of the Church in the world. Acts 8:3-8.)

*

The Apostle Peter introduced himself, in his "First Epistle General", only to hallow God the Father, and write of *"Jesus Christ, Whom having not seen, ye love . . . with Joy unspeakable and full of glory"* (1 Peter 1:7, 8).

*

"Joy", said young Percy Ainsworth, of our time, in a service to Jesus, our Lord, *"is one of life's deep things. It is one of the fathomless spontaneities of life. It is the soul's just response."*

*

A choice prayer, that some of us find easy to lodge in our memories is:

> Grant us, O Lord, the royalty of an inward happiness, and the serenity which comes from living close to Thee.
> *Daily renew in us the sense of Joy*! (R.L.S.)

Young people and old have echoed that prayer.

*

Jesus, as a young lad growing up in his family, would be familiar with the Psalmist's words recorded in the Old

Testament (which was the "Bible" He used): "Let all those who put their trust in Thee rejoice; *let them ever shout for joy*, because Thou defendest them: let them also that love Thy name *be joyful in Thee*" (Psalm 5:11).

Again and again as a young man, joining in worship, He must have heard the stirring words: "O come, let us sing unto the Lord: let us make *a joyful noise* to the Rock of our salvation. Let us come before His presence with thanksgiving, and make *a joyful noise unto Him with praise*" (Psalm 95:1, 2). "Solemn saints" through all Jesus's growing up, must have seemed wholly out of place in worship, as they would in personal religion. When it came time for Him to go about amongst men and women, as a Teacher, it seemed natural, now and again, to introduce a note of Joy. "A Man of Sorrows" He certainly was, at times; but though there was no sorrow like His on this earth, there was likewise no match for Him as "*the Man of Joy*"!

* * *

As Christian scholars or saints, we are not all a match for Dr James Denny, long remembered to have said: "There is not in the New Testament from beginning to end . . . a single word of despondency or gloom. It is the most bouyant, exhilarating, *and joyful book in the world*!"

*

In my own student days, the most read and treasured study book among us was Dr Harry Emerson Fosdick's *Manhood of the Master*. Study One started off with "The Master's Joy". Much of what the good Doctor had set down there, in that world renowned book, I find I marked in red ink. And the first such passage, I'm interested to note, was a collection of Jesus's words to His disciples whom He loved – and which were in turn meaningful to me as a young modern-day disciple: "These things have I spoken unto you that *My joy* may be in you, and that *your joy* may be full" (John 15:11).

* * *

"And why was He so joyous?" asked the good disciple, Fosdick. He answered his own question, and in italics: "*He had the most joyous idea of God that ever was thought of.*" He called God, "*Father*".

*

Said Jesus: "If ye keep My commandments, ye shall abide in My love; even as I have kept My Father's commandments, and abide in His love. These things I have spoken unto you, *that My joy might remain in you, and that your Joy might be full.*" (Words to His earliest disciples, recorded in John 15:10 and 11.)

*

As for Saul, he made havoc of the church, entering into every house, and haling men and women committed them to prison.

Therefore they that were scattered abroad went everywhere preaching the Word.

Then Philip went down to the city of Samaria, and preached Christ unto them.

And the people with one accord gave heed unto these things which Philip spake, hearing and seeing the miracles which he did . . . *And there was great joy in that city*. (Part of the early, costly witness of the Christian Church in the world – Acts 8:1-8.)

*

Prayer of early times – treasured for us in our later allegiance, reads:

"O Thou Who art the light of the minds that know
    Thee,
the joy of the hearts that love Thee, and
the strength of the wills that serve Thee;
Grant us so to know Thee
    That we may truly love Thee,
So to love Thee
    That we may freely serve Thee,
Whom to serve is perfect freedom:
    through Jesus Christ our Lord. AMEN."

                    St Augustine (A.D. 354-430)

Augustine was carrying forward the Apostle Peter's spirit
(as in the First Epistle General) to hallow the name of
God the Father, and of *"Jesus Christ, whom having not
seen, ye love . . . with joy unspeakable and full of glory"*
(1 Peter 1:7, 8).

    Out of his experience, the Rev. Percy Ainsworth re-
minded us: *"Joy is one of life's deep things. It is one of the
fathomless spontaneities."*

Prayers

Prayers and Praise to mingle with my own

Lord, help me to pray;
        to desire to pray,
        to delight to pray.
Make all my supplications *joyful* with faith,
        joyful with hope,
        joyful with love;
Joyful with Thine own Spirit interceding with
me . . .
Joyful in the fellowship of the prayers of the saints,
        and of Thy Church, above and below;

Through Him who in Heaven maketh intercession
       continually,
Thy Son, Jesus Christ our Lord. AMEN
        (Eric Milner-White, as Dean of York)

*

O God, when the heart is warmest,
And the head is clearest . . .
Give me to act:
To turn the purposes Thou formest
       Into fact.

                       Anon

In the morning

O God, source of this life's sustaining Joy, I praise
You, as the new day opens, for strength of body, and
freshness of mind.

Guide me in my choices, today, that I may do nothing in
the present that I shall be sorry for in the future.

Give me a teachable spirit and a joyous one. Enable me to
touch helpfully the lives of any I meet, in need of
courage and companionship.

In this age of tools and gadgets, it is all too easy to forget
that people matter more than things.

Save our daily relationships from being ruined by haste,
destroyed by prejudice, daunted by dullness.

Deliver me from all pretence, this day; from all pettiness
and foolish pride, I pray. Lighten the weight of my
labours with occasional laughter.

I thank You that I have worthwhile work to do; and need-
ful skill, and perseverance to do it. I think often of the
carpenter's bench at Nazareth.

Let the spirit that moved my young Master be mine.
Bless all closest to my life's service today; support

those who have needs beyond life's usual physical hurt, dullness, uncertainty, anxiety.

Sustain them through the late hours of this day and show me how I can help them to recover vanished Joy. For Christ's sake. AMEN.

*

Source of this Life's richest Joy, I bless Thee at day's beginning, that I do not journey alone. In this great world of men and women, that is impossible. I am never beyond the bounds of Thy Joy.

Again and again, I have forgotten this and been sorry for it. But in Thy mercy, Thou hast forgiven me. And now restored in body, mind, and spirit I give myself to Thy service once more.

And Thy great Joy – known first in Creation, when early on the morning stars sang together, and day and night alike moved out in response to Thy word – makes us endlessly rich! And something special is added, about the nature of Joy, as we listen to the words of our Lord, on His gift of Joy, recorded in the New Testament pages.

Accept for Thy Kingdom's sake, I pray, my readiness to receive, and share, all that makes up the "Good Harvest" of my Christian life. In daily witness, as I go about my normal affairs, let me not be counted among earth's "solemn saints". Let my unquestioned possession of the Joy of Christ be clear wherever life sets me to live.

Let me handle, as in Thy sight, all the practical tools of this day. Let me do my work, as faithfully as once Jesus did His serving Thy people coming to His craftsman's bench. As life rolls on, let us men and women responsible for the strong, joyous fabric of family life, look more and more to Thee for its secret. AMEN.

In the evening

that we have touched

O God, I rejoice that many of the people ~~with whom I've had dealings~~ today have ~~clearly~~ shown themselves to be Your people. I rejoice in their actions, more telling than words, in their steady values, and unselfishness.

I thank You for every piece of Joyous news passed on today; for those tending little children *'teaching out'* ~~gladly;~~ for good homemakers, and gardeners, whose colours and patterns of growth add something to us as we pass by, lifting our spirits.

I am the richer in my life, that many ~~folk~~ *people.* write good books; ~~that many write good letters; that many speak~~ *that many* ~~helpfully in public places; and serve good meals;~~ and do not forget to share the good things of life with the sick, and the ~~solitary,~~ *lonely* and the discouraged.

Bless, at this day's end, those who, for all their effort, have known failure today, in some issue they care about. Renew their courage when the new day comes.

Strengthen and encourage all who serve in public places – give them ~~good~~ *right* judgement, *in all that* and patience with human foolishness. Support especially all preacher~~s~~, Christian teachers, ~~pastor~~s, deacon~~esses~~, priests and nuns who serve Your Kingdom. In the Name of Christ, I pray.

AMEN.

*

~~Gracious God, our~~ Father, I praise Thee at the close of day, for friends and helpers close to my life. For ~~snippets of~~ good news; ~~for letters from afar;~~ for flowers that have today come to their season ~~of blooming~~. All these good gifts, I receive with Joy.

Let me, in my turn, bring something by way of enrichment into the lives of others about me.

I ~~give Thee thanks for books: on my own shelves; those offering me a wider selection in the Library; those lent~~

to me, as most precious possessions, by my friends. And I pray for all authors devoting their lives to making those books beautiful and useful experiences. Bless especially all who minister in this area of inspiration and information through Braille; through Large Print books; and through Talking Books.

And I thank Thee for the ongoing ministry of Thy Church here, and in Thy great world. Support now all who help to build Thy Kingdom on earth, with its Love, and lasting Joy. In the living Name of Christ our Lord. AMEN.

PEACE

The Harvest of the Spirit is Peace

In one of Paul's ever welcome Letters, preserved for us in the New Testament (Philippians 4:7) he writes of *"the Peace of God which passeth all understanding."* (A lovely description!)

Yet we go on trying to understand it – we need Peace so much. *In the world of Nature* that provides the background of our earth-life, storms of wind, rain, and at times, thunder, crash. *In our human relationships*, Peace seems even harder to establish. *And between nations* – as our newspapers and news bulletins daily remind us – the issue is a problem of still greater proportions. Occasionally, we are all but afraid to look, or to listen. Cinema films, and the smaller screens of T.V. within many of our homes, painfully arrest us. One thing is plain: the Peace that we seek in these various areas is at no time a static quality.

And when we come to make a spiritual quest, this we find is as true. Dr J.B. Phillips still tellingly reminds us: *"Peace with God* [to share his writing] *is not a static emotion. It is a positive gift which accompanies our living in harmony with God's plan. . . .* When we are *at one with Him in Spirit*, and at one with Him in purpose, we may know the deep satisfaction of the Peace of God."

Followers of Christ have at no time been immune where human struggle has entered. Nothing is more plain, as one reads the Book of Acts, the early story of the Church. It's a story of human involvement, even martyrdom. But they knew they had not been promised "a pleasant progress".

Their Lord's words, in prayer to God, were not to be forgotten. He loved those men. Said Jesus: "I pray *not* that Thou shouldest take them out of the world [with its disturbances] but that Thou shouldest *keep them from the evil*" [within the world] (John 17:15).

Dr Cleverley Ford, a modern commentator, in *Preaching through the Christian Year*, says: "*Peace, as the Bible understands it, is not an achievement of man's ingenuity, it is a gift which comes from God* . . . Peace is '*the harvest of the Spirit*'. It is not alone the harvest of intelligence. The roots of Peace reach down far deeper than the human mind, into the Love of God. . . . The call is to accept it and to practise it." Jesus said: "How blest are the peacemakers; God shall call them *His sons*" (John 1:13; New English Bible). (And, I dare to add, just as confidently, "His daughters"!)

One writes:

> And 'tis not the grave Peace of silence,
> Still'd lips, long face,
> Blank emptiness:
> *But the peace of a symphony*,
> Chord upon chord
> Built to a plan.

(Anon)

My first London Editor, and long-time friend, Dr Leslie Church, shared with me a peaceful memory of his dear mother: said he, "It chanced that I was free one New Year's Eve, and I went gladly to spend the last hour of the Year with her. She had been frail and lonely since my father died, but she never surrendered her faith to the storm. As I sat in the little room where she lay, our thoughts roamed back over the years.

"Memory after memory rose before us, till there came a point where I could go no further. She stretched out her hand to reach the watch, which she kept on the table beside her. 'It is a quarter to twelve', she said, which, being interpreted, meant, 'Let us be quiet a little, now . . .'

"It was very still in that little room, as still as I think it must be at the gate of Heaven. I suppose the minutes ticked away; I did not notice them – mine only to wait in a great silence. I looked at her face. A miracle had happened. I had never seen her like that before, though I think my father had. She was seventy years old, yet I saw her as though she had been but seventeen.

"I was in her little room, but she was, as the Scots say, 'far ben' in the secret place with God. Presently her thin hand reached out again, though there was no need for the watch. 'It's twelve o'clock, my boy', she said. 'A New Year has begun. God bless you.'

"As I stooped towards that shining face I knew the Master had spoken truth when He said, 'Happy are the pure in heart, for they shall see God.'

"She did not end that year on earth. Why should she? She had begun it in Heaven."

And that has remained clear ever since Dr Leslie shared it with me – a little word-picture of the Peace that can remain precious till the "end of the day".

*

The realities that we may know in this life – under the word "Peace", going on to "peaceable", "peacemakers" – are surprisingly many in our Bible. I can't tell how many; but I turned up my old, and much tattered *Cruden's Concordance*, left to me by a loved fellow deaconess with whom I trained; a long-time friend, and, as it happened, cousin of Irene Watts, with whom I shared a home and the rich things of our Faith, for fifty-one years, till Death through accident took her a few years ago. As Death took, even more suddenly, the owner of this old

Concordance, now open before me as I write, Sister Edna Lenna Button – "Buttons" to those of us who were greatly enriched by her sharing.

She had set her heart on further studies in one of the Colleges in peaceful England, for which I had encouraged her to put her name down. But war had come soon after she set foot in England; so that she soon found herself in the uniform, and hospital service of the WAAF (Women's Auxiliary Air Force), as a medical orderly. But in early September, enemy bombs fell on peaceful Kent, and on Buttons' air hospital. She managed to get everyone she was responsible for down into the simple trenches – but blast caught her! "Year by year", as someone had said, "we find we are being led forward to a life too big for this world to contain", I wrote and dedicated a book to her memory. But we could not have guessed that death would have come so soon to "Buttons". With a quick mind, boundless energy, and a twinkle in her eye, she had endeared herself to many youthful spirits. Guides, Cubs and Brownies loved her. Never waiting for votes of thanks, no job was beneath her dignity, and a few in the immediate tasks outside her ability. We had seen her prepare delectable camp meals out of next to nothing, or half-sole shoes, coax old clothes into renewed life and freshness, prepare and lead youth services of worship, or with pen and crayons turn out jolly posters that were the envy and delight of all who saw them. She was always making something. God lent her a valiant spirit, a good pair of hands, and a self-forgetfulness.

Few, I am sure, came to know "Buttons" so well as those who turned into some long lane of darkness, loneliness, or sickness – and on the urgent basis of their need discovered her unassuming yet amazing understanding.

I am but one of many who have lived better, because she called me "friend".

She is not dead. How could she be? For such beings, life goes on,

> Out of the city's shadow they are gone,
> Out of Life's dimness into God's own day;
> Within, we weep, then front the dawn and pray,
> And strengthened, to the unfinished work pass on.

* * *

Her well-used Concordance offers a note on the word "Peace": (1) There is Peace with God; (2) There is Peace with ourselves, or our own consciences; (3) There is Peace with men and women – mutual concord; especially Peace between Christians; (4) Peace, as opposed to war, when a State, or Country, enjoys public tranquility; (5) There is the Peace of Nature – of trees, hills, lakes and skies. We all like to see these out.

A modern poet, Margaret Read – unknown to me for anything else she has written – says simply and tellingly:

> When in the closeness of a friend I know
> *A feeling of great peace*,
> Then I am sure that in the afterworld
> It will not cease.
> In that glad moment I am filled
> With awe that I may see
> A glimpse of great eternities
> That are to be.

To read, and maybe memorize

Old Testament

"*Agree with God, and be at Peace*: thereby good will come to you." (Job 22:21; R.S.V.)

New Testament

Paul wrote, in a letter long cherished by his Christian friends: "Have no anxiety about anything, but in everything by prayer and supplication with thanksgiving let your requests be made known to God. And *the Peace of God, which passes all understanding*, will keep your hearts and your minds in Christ Jesus" (Philippians 4:7; R.S.V.).

> Sing, soul of mine, this day of days,
>   The Lord is risen!
> Toward the sunrising set thy face.
>   The Lord is risen!
> Behold He giveth strength and grace;
> For darkness, light; for mourning, praise;
> For sin, His holiness; for conflict, *Peace*.

(Anon)

*

> To my weariness, O Lord,
>   vouchsafe Thou rest;
>   to my exhaustion
>   renew Thou strength.
> Supply me with healthy sleep,
> *And to pass through this night*
>   *without fear*.

(Anon)

Seeking Peace – and sharing Peace, I voice the prayer attributed to St Francis:

> *Lord, make me an instrument of Thy Peace.*
> Where there is hatred, let me sow love;
> Where there is injury, pardon;
> Where there is discord, union;
> Where there is doubt, faith;
> Where there is despair, hope;
> Where there is darkness, light;
> Where there is sadness, joy;
> For Thy mercy and for Thy truth's sake. AMEN.

"Bishop Dibelius, in Berlin, could have had *peace* with the East German Communist regimes. For that nothing much was required – just a little adjustment of his Christian convictions. But he chose to follow the way of conscience and conviction and chose, not the peace of quiet compromise, but *the Peace of the Passion*" (The Rev. David H.C. Read, D.D.).

*

"A few days later," Dr Read continued, in his book *I Am Persuaded*, "I found myself running to keep another appointment. As I dived down the subway I just missed a North-bound express and began to pace the platform. It would have been a moment for quiet reflection – but the 14th Street Subway Station is not exactly the Taj Mahal, and I was soon part of a growing crowd of tense, impatient, restless citizens in a wilderness of chewing-gum machines. Trains clattered by on other lines, brakes squealed, harsh voices argued, and anxious heads peered into the dark tunnel as if to extract the coaches for which we were all feverishly waiting.

"Suddenly I felt that someone was looking at me. I

turned and met the wide open, unblinking blue eyes of a six-month-old infant, lying *peacefully* in his mother's arms. He was completely undisturbed by the noise, and in those blue eyes there was not the slightest reflection of the nervous anxious glances all around him. It was as if he said to me, 'What are you all worried about? . . . Look; I'm in my mother's arms and I trust her completely. *Have you nothing to rest on, no one to trust?*'"

"Verily I say unto you", repeating the words of the Master, "whosoever shall not receive the Kingdom of God as a little child shall in no wise enter therein." "Why are ye so fearful? *Have faith in God.*"

*

"*And the Peace of God which passeth all understanding, shall keep your hearts and minds through Christ Jesus*" (Philippians 4:7).

Prayers to mingle with mine

In the morning

Gracious God, my Father, as I open my eyes this morning, I remember before You how many lack *the Peace I know*. Deliver me, here and now, from vague goodwill. Some live in faraway lands, where I have never been, and whose setting I cannot visualize. It is not easy to remember their daily needs. Bless the ongoing work of societies in every part of the world, who faithfully remember them, and continually do what they can, to keep us all aware.

Support those who give personal service in strange and distressing situations overseas – those who must bear heavy organizing responsibilities, often in an unhelpful climate and using a strange tongue. Guide, and strengthen, I pray, all whose service makes special demands on them – doctors, nurses, chemists and organizers, packers and distributors. Keep them faithful and alert. Uphold all who serve through the United Nations, that difficult and tangled situations may be wisely resolved. Guide all who meanwhile must serve where there is no peace.

Enable me, here today, to go forth, *with Your Peace in my heart, to do gladly what I can, in this needy world. For Christ's Sake*. AMEN.

In the evening

At day's end, O God, I rejoice that You have given me, as ever, a sense of Your nearness. Today, You have lent me my body for service, my mind for thought, and have kept alive within my spirit, *a lasting Peace*. And no two days are ever wholly alike. I rejoice in good surprises: letters and phone-calls, photos and magazines from afar. I give thanks for fresh flowers that have opened out; for the fun of children, and friends; for fresh ideas – and for good food, and rest at nightfall.

Be especially near this night, to any known to me who are sick, or uncertain in their actions; to any suffering loneliness or a sense of futility. I would speak their names in Your Holy Presence, as I settle to sleep.

We are all Your earth-children, with our many and various needs. Support us, I pray, guide us, forgive us, and bring us safely – with fresh expectations and vital faith – into the new days ahead. And set some renewing laughter on our lips, for the enrichment of our life together. In Christ's Name. AMEN.

In the morning – at home – surrounded with thy peace

I speak my heart's thankfulness, for ....
and ....

I rejoice in the simple strengths of Life that fortify me . . .

I pause in Thy presence to note the beauty, colour and shape of common things.

Hold me faithful, this day. AMEN.

PATIENCE

The Harvest of the Spirit is Patience

For the first time I can remember, I have been hunting through my several dictionaries to see what they have to say about **Patience**. Perhaps it was too much to expect to find something fresh, but typical was what one of the most comprehensive, *The Britannica World Language Dictionary*, had to say. (Yet it was limp, colourless, woefully dull, and negative!) *"Patience"*, it said, *"is the quality or habit of enduring without complaint."*

I turned to my New Testament, but, as it happened, made an unfortunate start. I'd always counted James a very practical man, but here, he merely broke into the matter with a question: *"Have you heard of the Patience of Job?"* (James 5:11). I had to reply: "Well, yes, I have." As a young student I once had a whole term's lectures on him and his Patience – and it took the whole united patience we young people could muster, to see it to the end! I have since discovered in the biblical account of poor Job's problems, dramatic qualities, even some attractive poetry – perhaps one has to be mature to read his book, and I had started too young.

Not surprisingly, my most valuable discovery awaited me in the New Testament in John's lovely reference to *"the patience of Jesus Christ"* (in Revelation 1:9). This was a reality unsurpassed in this earth. Men and women had seen it again and again, gloriously manifested in everyday dealings. Mary Magdalene had besmirched her womanhood; but her personality did not end there. A new, and beautiful, Mary Magdalene emerged – *through the Patience of Christ*!

Peter, the blundering fisherman, at the end of several

years of close company, three times over grievously denied his Master – but even that was not the end of things. In time, he was forgiven three times over, and renewed, *through the Loving Patience of the Risen Christ*!

And this marvel is still operative in human lives, in situations as difficult as those confronted in the experiences of Mary Magdalene and of Simon Peter – lovable people, both of them – as time went by. But the secret of such, who held a unique place in the glorious ministry of the early Church, was *not in a definition* – but in *the loving patience of Christ himself*! **And it still is**!

One of the most moving modern instances that I have come across once came as my friend, Rene, and I sat in our sunny lounge, listening to a longtime YWCA prisoner of the Japanese, on a visit she paid us when released from a wretched camp in Batavia. (And she gave me leave to share it.) "There, in the camp", said she, remembering those grim days, "was a young Dutch woman whose first little one had been born after the husband had been imprisoned.

"The little girl was lovely, and quite naturally, the young mother longed for her husband to have the joy of seeing her. For some months she was at a loss to know how it could be achieved. But her loving patience persisted.

"The birthday of the young husband approached; and after much thought, she made a request to the Japanese authority for permission to take the child to the barbed wire of the prison camp, where her husband was held, and to send her in to greet him on his birthday.

"There was great jubilation when the Japanese officer, with trepidation, gave consent for the mother to do that. Friends in the camp heard the news, and in time – having offered little gifts out of their poverty, to help the baby 'look nice' – saw both set off.

"It involved a walk of some distance to the agreed

barrier. The mother herself was not allowed to see her husband, but with *the courage of loving patience*, trusting in the innate gentleness towards children characteristic of the Japanese, she handed over her baby to the Japanese guard, who took her on to her overjoyed father!

"Meanwhile, the long moments ticked by.

"*Later, the guard brought the little one safely back to her waiting mother*", said our friend, herself so lately back from that grim wartime situation.

"*What loving patience was there – of the very Spirit of Christ!*"

* * *

"The Love of which I speak", said Dr J.B. Phillips, in his translation of 1 Corinthians 1:3 "*is slow to lose patience* – it looks for a way of being constructive; it is neither anxious to impress, nor does it cherish inflated ideas of its own importance . . . Love knows no limits to its endurance, no end to its trust, no fading of its hope. *It can outlast anything.*"

To read and maybe memorize

Old Testament

Fret not thyself because of evildoers, neither be thou envious against the workers of iniquity. For they shall soon be cut down like the grass, and wither as the green herb.

Trust in the Lord, and do good; so shalt thou dwell in the land, and verily thou shalt be fed.

Delight thyself in the Lord; and He shall give thee the desires of thine heart . . .

Rest in the Lord, and wait patiently for Him. (Psalm 37:1-7)

New Testament

"Having heard the word, keep it, and bring forth fruit with Patience." (Luke 8:15)

*

Paul wrote: "We then, as workers together with Him, beseech you also that ye receive not the grace of God in vain. For He saith, 'I have heard thee in a time accepted, and in the day of salvation have I succoured thee: behold, *now* is the accepted time; behold, *now* is the day of salvation. Giving no offence in anything, that the ministry be not blamed; but in all things approving ourselves as *the ministers of God, in much Patience*.'" (2 Corinthians 6:1)

*

In a poem called "At the Place of the Sea", Annie Johnson Flint, a Christian who knew her dramatic Old Testament history, in relation to all time (re-read Exodus 13:17-22; and 14:1-31), wrote for us each:

> Have you come to the Red Sea place in your life,
> Where, in spite of all you can do,
>   There is no way out, there is no way back,
> There is no other way but through?
>   Then wait on the Lord, with a trust serene,
> Till the night of your fear is gone;
>   He will send the winds, He will heap the floods,
> When He says to your soul, "*Go on!*"

"*God works for our unexpected deliverance, at times – by way of Patience.*"

That was the discovery of sensitive James Montgomery, who wrote for us over four hundred hymns, including some very well known ones such as "Angels from the

realms of glory", "Hail to the Lord's Anointed" and
*"Prayer is the soul's sincere desire, Uttered or unexpressed,
The motion of a hidden fire That trembles in the breast."*

* * *

Not to the wise, O Lord, nor to the prudent,
　　Dost Thou reveal Thyself, nor to the art
Of the logician keen, and coldly student,
　　But to *the patience of the pure in heart*.

Low is the lintel of Thy Truth, and lowly
　　Mortals must bend who fain would see Thy face;
Slow from the darkness dawns the day, and slowly
　　Sinners ascend into Thy dwelling-place.

(Unknown)

*

O Master,
　　Thou Who walked on Galilee,
　　O Master,
　　Thou Who conquered mighty things,
　　Did small things vex and trouble Thee?

*

Of his Christian experience – the poet says:
　　Let no man think that sudden, in a minute,
　　All is accomplished, and the work is done –
　　*Though with thine earliest dawn thou shouldst
　　　begin it,
　　Scarce were it ended in thy setting sun.*

(F.W. Myers)

*

"Keep me from turning back", are the words of one –

"My hand is on the plough, my faltering hand:
But all in front of me is untilled land.
Keep me from turning back,
The shares with rust are spoiled – and yet – and
    yet –
My God! My God! Keep me from turning back."

*

Let nothing disturb thee,
  Nothing affright thee.
All things are passing.
    God never changeth.
Patience gains all things.
Who hath God wanteth nothing.
    Alone God sufficeth.   (*St Teresa of Avila*)

*

Over the years, James Montgomery happened on difficult situations, but he was again and again delivered, *by waiting patiently on God*. What he wrote of one such experience, was true of very many. And he wrote gratefully:

For hither, from my native clime,
The Hand that leads Orion forth,
And wheels Arcturus round the north,
Brought me.

It could be a good thing whenever, as now, our thoughts are on patience, to ponder the words of Polly in Lucas Malet's story. Do you remember them? "What does one end by doing when all the best is taken away from one, when life has grown trivial – stunted and narrow; when the sun of one's happiness has set?" To that, her old uncle replied: "After a time, Polly, not all at once – that would be asking too much of poor human nature – but after a time, my dear, *one lights a candle called Patience, and guides one's steps by that.*"

Polly continued: "Did your candle burn brightly at first?"

"No," he answered, "it burned very badly at first, did my candle; guttered, had thieves in the wick. And meanwhile I stumbled pretty freely. It has burned brighter as time has gone by . . . burns brightly enough now . . . *Try to light your candle of Patience, Polly, remembering that you are not alone.*"

*

Speaking on one occasion to a number of people, each as deeply involved in life as we all are, Dr Jowett said a striking thing which I've never forgotten: "*Patience is there – but it is not lit up!*" The Patience of Christ is always lit up!

*

God who a thousand years doth wait
To work a thousandth part of Thy great plan,
In me create
A humble, patient heart.

(*George MacDonald*)

*

C.S. Lewis says: "We may ignore, but we can nowhere evade, the presence of God. The world is crowded with Him. He walks everywhere *incognito*. And the *incognito* is not always hard to penetrate. The real labour is to remember *to attend.*"

*

"*We and God have business with each other*; and in opening ourselves to His influence our deepest destiny is fulfilled."

(*William James*)

Prayers, to add to my own

In the morning

O God, my Father, Creator and Giver of all good, Light streams across my room, as this new day comes. I cannot imagine what its hours hold, though nothing can take You by surprise.

In this quiet, and loved place, I would drop all haste, and bow my head, thankful for *Your good gift of Patience*.

Bless me this day, and all with whom I have to do. Especially, I pray, any who seek their own will, and are unwilling to bend to Your greater glory.

Support us this day, I pray, in any unexpected event – anything involving the hurt of others. *Deliver us from unhappy haste*, if we have to mingle with crowds.

Let us see how things *sacred and secular are helpfully tied together*, in our ongoing earth-life. We see this secret in the choice life of Jesus, our Master.

Enable us to show His tenderness for little children; for growing life of grass and garden; for the sick, and the easily cast aside. Give us His sweet approachableness, His gentle touch, His healing compassion.

Let us rejoice in things of beauty, as we go on our way; let us use our skills, to enrich others' lives; to share our books, music, and art, and discoveries in travel.

It is often easier to dream of great events, than to be continually involved in small and daily essentials. *Let our own Patience today, issue in real helpfulness*. AMEN.

In the evening

O God, I can never be glad enough that You have given me my home. And that I have spent so many happy hours here.

I am enriched again and again, by those of my friends

and neighbours who cross my doorstep; by those who share happy experiences; who bring me of the fruits and flowers of their gardens; and occasionally step in to share a meal or a gale of laughter.

I bless You for helpful ones ever ready to keep an eye on my home; to bring in my mail, when I am on holiday. Save me from self-centredness.

You have lent me my body, for life here and now; my mind for lively thought and awareness; and my questing spirit, that I may lay hold of the lasting values of Jesus Christ, my Lord. I bow my head in thankfulness, at day's end. AMEN.

At any time

O God our Father, we give Thee thanks for Life; for rising from sleep refreshed each morning. For the clothes we put on, and the food we eat; *for the patience* of those with whom we share the tasks of the day; and the ease at day's end. AMEN. (*William Barclay*)

*

Dear Lord, make me *to be patient* . . . towards all unlovely people, so that they may catch just a glimpse in me, maybe, of the beauty of Jesus, my Master.

May I listen to their sorrows; and try to understand something of their anxieties.

Use me this day, to bring light and peace to hearts that are full of darkness and distress.

O Lord, use me and guide me, for Thy sake. AMEN.
(*Frank Doubleday*)

*

Father, in this hour, grant me *a lively patience* with those whose views are different from my own. Clarify our values; let us enjoy to show to others, a sincere respect.

Grant me courage to withhold approval of that which is unworthy, unjust, unkind.

Quicken my love for all that is joyous, good and true, displayed in the lives of others.

Give me *the patience needed* for a daily, steadfast witness to the things of thine Eternal Kingdom. In the Name of Christ, my Saviour. AMEN.

*

Gracious God, creator of all good, and lovely gifts; forgive me if I have lacked *time and patience to pause*, and rejoice in the colour and shape of things.

Give me a lively interest in the purpose for which Thou hast set them here.

Give me a goodly concern for their protection, and sharing – trees, seashores and living, rare gifts of Nature.

Bestow Thy special gift of Joy on all who are generous; all who give humbly, without show, not letting their left hand know what their right hand doeth.

Bless all who have nothing of a material kind to offer, but are rich in out-reaching Love. Bless the hospitable of heart and home, I pray – and let me learn their art of natural sharing. With the spirit of all true Marthas and Marys who still welcome their Living Lord. AMEN.

KINDNESS

The Harvest of the Spirit is Kindness

The word "kindness", and its kin – "kind-hearted", "kindleness" – seem always to walk with gentle steps, and speak in the same way. It doesn't seem likely that one can show kindness, or receive it from another, in a harsh, thoughtless, demanding mood. It's a word of the heart, an expression of love. "Kindness" seems always to find a way to do something about a situation – and often in a very personal, surprising way. Kindness makes a great difference to things. It's a pleasure to recall instances of "kindness" that, over the years, have come to oneself and to others.

A writer in a journal that comes to my desk, lately took a book by Dornford Yates (*As Berry and I Were Saying*) from his civic library, in the belief that it was a thriller. He found instead that the author had given him what he called "a rather fascinating hotch-potch of reminiscences, mainly of his career at the Bar.

"But one of his tales", he added, "impressed me so much that I am going to condense it for you. During a prize-giving at Harrow, he was astonished to hear his name called by the headmaster, Joseph Wood.

"He knew he had not won a prize, and had not spruced himself up to go to the dais to receive one; but all untidy as he was, he braved the watching twelve hundred eyes and went to the desk and back.

"The book burned his hands, as he knew he had not earned it; so, when all was over, he made his way to the dais again, and haltingly explained the position to his painfully pompous form-master, who said: 'Ah, Head-master, there seems to have been some mistake. This, ah, boy, is not entitled to a prize, and so he's brought the book back.'

"Wood took the book from his hands, and looked at the grubby boy before him, who never felt so much ashamed. Then he smiled, and gave him the book back. 'Take it back, my boy,' he said smilingly, 'you'll be worth it one day.'

"There", adds my commentator, "spoke a very great gentleman."

I can only add, in my own words: "*There spoke Kindness!*"

And it was something that the boy – as we have seen – grew up remembering all his life!

I can't believe that any one of us is ever in a position where it is never possible to show kindness. Perhaps that is one of God's good reasons why *we are set down, shoulder to shoulder somewhere in this great world, to do the best we can, to grow up together*! For, looking back, with what life has taught me, I feel sure that we can't, any of us, grown up into rounded personalities, without Kindness!

* * *

The New Testament word is *crestotes*, scholars tell us; and that rubs shoulders closely all the way with "goodness". It's a lovely word – "a particular Bible word, that does not occur in secular Greek", Dr William Barclay claimed.

There is a fine use of this word, meaning "Kind", in a New Testament reference that ties up with Jesus's early carpentering days; and His later compassionate ministry to men and women. The first awaits us in Matthew 11:30, of the New English Bible, in the words of Jesus: "My yoke is *chrestos*, that is 'kind', translated 'easy'" (N.E.B. "good to bear"). He is saying to those who would follow Him, that His "yoke of discipleship" does not chafe, or irritate.

(It is as if the Carpenter is running His fingers over a yoke He has just turned out from His workshop, and is speaking to some possible customer who has come in from a pastoral part of the country, "Look, this yoke is *chrestos*, kind!")

It is a lovely word, close to life, tied lastingly into action. *It matches human need* – as does the yoke to the simple farmer who needs to turn his soil if he is to raise a crop, and, at the turn of the season, have corn to sell, to support his home and family.

Jesus was see often to have offered kindness of Himself, as He did to the sinning woman who came in where He was taking a meal – and anointed His feet. It was a truly understanding, gracious thing to do (Luke 7:36-50). "Jesus lavished *His 'Kindness'* on all He met, except the self-righteous and self-satisfied", says Jean Coggan, wife of the former Archbishop of Canterbury. "Even to them, His words of rebuke were *kind*," she adds, "in that they were meant to bring them to repentance and faith."

And Paul – as his Christian life and understanding widened out – could not hold his heart from repeating its lasting worth. To his friends in Corinth, he wrote unforgettably: "*Love is very patient, very kind*" (Moffatt's Translation, 1 Corinthians 13:4).

And so it is. He never wrote a truer word!

* * *

And to this day, no one of us need look up his or her dictionary for the definition that lodges there. Born into a Christian home, I never had such a need – my father and mother, from our first moment of meeting, had each a pair of "kind hands". And countless other little children have been born to know a like experience, both in our country and in others as fortunate. (*The very word "Kindness" is almost a Christian word to us*.) So that when the poet-hymn-writer Margaret Cropper, born in 1886, wanted to engage children in song, she wrote:

> *Jesus' hands were kind hands*, doing good to all,
> healing pain and sickness, blessing children small,
> washing tired feet, and saving those who fall;
> Jesus' hands were kind hands, doing good to all.

Together with a second verse it appears in the latest hymnal to come my way – a fine music copy with a red cover, its gold title in bold capitals: WITH ONE VOICE. A hymn book for all the Churches. With New Zealand Supplement. So I have, Sunday by Sunday, a chance to hear the children sing the second verse:

> Take my hands, Lord Jesus, let them work for You,
> make them strong and gentle, *kind in all I do*;
> let me watch You, Jesus, till I'm gentle, too,
> *till my hands are kind hands*, quick to work for You.

But there are many little ones in our world who have no such experience from birth, and must be brought to it by someone outside the family. A missionary story I know shares this reality.

A young Indian minister was deeply concerned for his people. In the villages in his care were many members of the leather-working caste, recent converts, in whom the fear of evil spirits was not far off. When a feared epidemic struck not far from the minister's house, he nursed them himself, sitting up with them at night, teaching the relatives how to prepare a proper diet, and attending to the necessary sanitary precautions. And largely by his efforts, the epidemic was stopped. He wanted to get his people to be willing to receive the protection of inoculation. But most of them were afraid of offending the old gods, and of anything new.

"I went with him to one village", says the missionary sister who tells the story. "We went into the 'school', a small shed with mud walls and thatched roof, and tried to persuade the people to come. But they huddled together some distance away, blankly refusing something of which they were afraid. It seemed that the minister would have to give it up.

"But he went on to the verandah, called the children, and began to play a game. He has four children of his own, and is their much-loved playmate. Soon, he was sitting on a low stool, in his spotless white clothes, and his lap was full of grubby, smelly, eager little children. He began with a story, and presently turned it into a story-game. In the middle of the game he rolled up his sleeve and turned to me. Seeing what he wanted, I gave him the inoculation he had been meaning to have at home that night. The fun got faster and merrier.

"Again and again, up came a grubby small arm, and (carefully choosing a very sharp needle) I inoculated that. And the fun went on, till soon every child in that group had received the necessary dose, and not one had even whimpered. The grown-ups, more and more intrigued, kept pressing nearer and nearer, and when the children were done, we turned to them, and they came to share in the game.

"A Government vaccinator, faced with that situation, and cut off from the villagers by caste, fastidiousness, and fear", added the sister, "would have had no chance but to go away, leaving the people unprotected, a danger to themselves, and everyone else."

* * *

How right Paul was: "Love is very patient, *very kind*" (Corinthians 13:4; Moffatt translation).

To read or maybe memorize

Old Testament

Blessed be the Lord: for He hath shewed me His marvellous *Kindness*! (Psalm 31:21)

New Testament

Be kindly affectioned one to another with brotherly love . . . Not slothful in business; fervent in spirit. (Romans 12:10-11)

*

Christianity taught us to care. Caring is the greatest thing. Caring matters most. (*Baron von Hügel*)

> While some of my brothers
> In misery lie,
> I cannot pray "Father",
> And pass them by.
> Of what use is doctrine,
> Or dogma, or creed,
> If I lack awareness
> Of my brothers' need?

(Anon)

(Go over the story of The Good Samaritan in Luke 10:30-36.)

Today, I shall stretch forth my hands,
And I shall share
My bounty with the world's less fortunate;
I shall have a part in the teaching of the world;
The feeding of its poor,

The clothing of its naked, shivering ones.
With my help shall its tortured flesh be healed;
Then – only then,
Can I endure my warmth and light and food,
Then only shall I dare to kneel and pray.

(Anon)

*

This is the miracle I seek,
O Living Christ,
Your strength and purpose in my hands,
Your kindness in my voice,
Within my heart Your certainty of God,
Your love for all mankind.

(Anon)

*

I count love by the daily round
Of little services designed
To make life beautiful and kind.

(Anon)

Prayers to mingle with my own

Giver of the increasing good,
take my thanks for all that has made me what I am;
for all my yesterdays, their disciplines, their pleasant
    songs,
my unanswered prayers, even those whelming hours
in which I have seen how frail I am without Thee.
And when the sorrow comes, with a new duty, a new
    truth,
may the door of my mind be open,
And I at the door to bid them welcome. AMEN.

(*Alistair MacLean*)

*

O God, Thou art the Breath
    That stirs the forest trees;
Thou art the mystic Silence
    Of the hills;
Thou art the Light
    That floods all lands and seas;
Thou, O my Lord,
    Art Light and Life to me. AMEN.

(Unknown)

*

O God, who so fillest all things that they only thinly veil Thy presence; we adore Thee in the beauty of the world, in the goodness of human hearts and in the thought within the mind. We praise Thee for the channels through which Thy grace can come to us; sickness and health, joy and pain, freedom and necessity, sunshine and rain, life and death. AMEN. (*Dr W.E. Orchard*)

*

O God, my Father Eternal, it is wonderful to know that
    Thou art in charge of this world –
so many changes have come since I was young – some of
    them hard to accept;
so many companions of my years are no longer here – I
    seem at times so much alone;
so many frightening events get into the headlines of the
    paper, that I tremble for the world.
Yet I know that nothing can happen to any of us, without
    Thy knowledge – no new experience can take Thee by
    surprise;
        so I trust Thee utterly. AMEN.

74

In the morning

Lord of Life, and gracious Heart of all true Kindness. I step out into this new day, with eager expectations. And my heart is full of thanks. I ask for Thy special support for any required to face hard tasks this day. I know that some will deal with difficult children; some now are puzzled how to handle defiant youth. These need not only special strengths, but out-matching Kindness. And You are the source of this lovely quality. You are truly the One God – in Whom we rightfully "live and move, and have our being" (Acts 17:28).

Let me walk humbly today, simply beneath this sky, reaching out with kindly encouragement to any I meet who are in special need of what help I can give.

Hold in Your kindly keeping any who have allowed themselves to become cynical. Any who have taken refuge in their natural shyness.

Guide all who work chiefly with their minds, and their imagination; bless, no less, those who work with their bodies, through sensitive and sturdy strength. All who serve, day after day, alone. All who mingle with fellow workers.

Guide especially those in postions of authority – let them learn how best to spell out Kindness.

And let us all today serve, when perhaps only Thou canst see, as faithfully as though all the world saw. In the Name of Christ, our Lord, the Carpenter, Who made of His Earth-Life such a triumphant thing. AMEN.

In the evening

Gracious Lord of Life, in its infinite variety and wonder, I hush my heart at day's end – to express thanks for the rich *Harvest* I have gathered over the years. Your great, unmeasured Love; Joy; Peace; and ongoing Patience. So generous beyond all human imagining!

And now comes Your bountiful gift of Kindness. There is no God like unto You! And still, my "Good Harvest of The Spirit" is not complete. I rejoice in this certainty, made known to me through Jesus Christ my Saviour and Master. It is wonderful to spend here a day like this – in a life like this – in a world like this!

And with the passing of Time, let me go on gathering in "The Harvest of the Spirit", that, in Time and Eternity's boundless measure, is Your Gift! In humility, and in wonder, I bow here my head, and my heart, in Thy Holy Presence! AMEN.

At night

Looking back over today, O Lord, I am led to offer Thee praise –
    for the promise of the morning;
    for *the kindness of friends*;
    for the truth of the Gospel, ever sure,
No tongue can bring to Thee worthy praise –
    let my life out-match my words;
    let my heart be always toward Thee;
    let my Christian witness be consistent,
So bless my coming in at evening, as Thou didst bless my going out –
    and in Thy mercy, remember —————————————
    and ————————— and —————————
AMEN.

*

Gracious God, forgive the haste and thoughtlessness of some of our prayers. It is a mercy that You do not answer them – for many are so shortsighted.

We lack experience to look far enough ahead. We are not generous enough to measure what answers to the small personal prayers we offer, might mean to others.

Mercifully, we are all of Thy family, on earth – *and in Thy keeping*. And for this we give thanks, in the Name of Christ, Who trusted Thee – even on the Cross. AMEN.

GOODNESS

"The Harvest of the Spirit is Goodness"

Here I am back under my own kindly roof, after my latest trip to London. I have returned with a sense of enrichment – and a lively desire to write about "Goodness". In my many busy journeys around the world, I've met it again and again; but have not written about it especially, until now. "Goodness" so easily sinks into "goodi-goodiness" in some people's reckoning – which is a disaster, and a disservice to this lovely word, so gracious it is, so happy, so healthy, so gifted, so glorious! (We all know it when we see it, I don't need to go to my dictionary for a definition – and when, out of curiosity, I do, I find it only says at length what I already know.)

On a precious last, sunny afternoon – and it was precious, the Spring weather being all the way through so poor – I went across a part of London I don't know well, to the tall-towered Church of "St Sepulchre-without-Newgate", as it is called. I had read somewhere during the year about "The Musicians' Memorial Chapel" – and to go there was a most rewarding experience.

My eyes met at once some beautiful stained glass windows, many reaching back in time, but with a goodly number of modern ones. It was early in the afternoon, with few people about, and so, beautifully quiet. The sun coming in was helpful. Each of the thirty choir chairs, I saw at once, had a beautifully handworked "kneeler" in coloured wools – bearing, neatly wrought, the name of the musician to be memorialized. I looked at each, knowing many of the names, and over the years, with my musical friend, Rene, I had heard many of them perform: Dame

Myra Hess, Julius Katchen, etc. But, as it happened, the very first chair I paused before, was that of Kathleen Ferrier. Rene and I had long rejoiced in her gifts on those travel occasions when we heard her sing, treasured her records; and listened to her voice over the air from Britain.

But Kathleen Ferrier was far more than a glorious voice, the like of which we may not hear again in this generation. She was a person young, fresh, beautiful, gifted, *and good*! Which also meant, in the words of one of her biographers, that "she was as brave in the face of vicissitude" – she died early of cancer – "as she was happy in all weathers – 'Blow the wind southerly'. She possessed a gift which radiated happiness. Her personal qualities even transcended her art, for great though she was as a singer, she was greater still as Kathleen Ferrier."

A lesser spirit might have paraded her gifts, might have given herself airs – but not Kathleen Ferrier. "Nobody", added her biographer, "could hope to be a friend of hers who was tinged in the slightest degree with meanness, deceit, or affectation."

Bruno Walter shared with her admirers, in writing, a lovely example of her unaffected spirit. On one occasion when she was in America, he chanced to be very busy with music in New York. He could not – to his loss – play host to her in his Los Angeles home; but he allowed her the use of it. "When we came home after she had left", he wrote, "our faithful domestic helpers, a married Austrian couple, told us that Kathleen, on her free evenings, used to call them to the music room, where she sat down at the piano, shed her shoes, and sang to them to their heart's desire, and of course, to their utter delight."

She allowed herself no parade, gave herself no airs. She didn't need to – she was too natural and good, for that!

* * *

The Musicians' Memorial Chapel was finer, and larger than I'd expected, and I spent quite a length of time there. As I came out, I noticed that a pleasant woman had just entered the big Church of St Sepulchre. As there was no other person there, I spoke to her, asking, "Do you know this old church?" "No," she replied, "I just happened to be passing, and I thought I'd step in."

I told her then – still in church whispers – where I came from, and about the names I'd copied down, beginning with that of Kathleen Ferrier. "Don't go", I said, "without allowing yourself to spend a little time in the Memorial Chapel."

I moved then to see other features of the old church, and to pick up a neat folder about its bells.

The time came for me to leave, and I stepped out on to the wide sunny pavement, hoping I might learn from somebody passing, that I could walk back by a shorter route than the taxi had taken when I'd come. There weren't many passers-by, but at that moment, an elderly gentleman, who looked likely to know his way about, approached, and I ventured my question. Yes, he did know exactly how I could get to one end of Fleet Street!

I had just thanked him, and he'd left, when the pleasant body I'd spoken to about The Musicians' Memorial Chapel came rushing out. "Oh, don't go yet", she said, "till I've properly thanked you!" (And she gave me a great kiss!) "The chance to see inside The Memorial Chapel", she said, *"has just made my day!"*

"And mine, too", I said.

To read, maybe to memorize

Old Testament

My faithful Concordance tells me that the word "Goodness" is to be found over thirty times in the Old Testament

– a time or two, reaching out to "Goodlier", "Goodliest" and "Goodliness" (A.V.).

Goodness is a lovely, dependable quality, as the brief prayer of the Psalmist that I have chosen shows:

> Remember not the sins of my youth, or my
> transgressions;
> according to Thy steadfast love remember me,
> for Thy goodness' sake, O Lord!
>
> (Psalm 25:7, R.S.V.)

New Testament

Here we read: "He also told the following parable to certain persons *who were sure of their own goodness*, and looked down upon everybody else" (Luke 18:9, Moffatt. Read on.)

*

One who fashioned a "Fifth Century Collect" gave us these moving words:

> O God, bless all who worship Thee,
> From the rising of the sun
> Unto the going down of the same,
> *Of Thy goodness, give us*,
> With Thy love, inspire us.

On my shelves are a number of books by the valiant J.B. Phillips, beginning with *Letters to Young Churches*, a translation of the New Testament epistles. In time came *The Gospels – translated into Modern English*, to be followed to my welcoming shelves by *Your God is too small*, and *Four Prophets* and *Ring of Truth*.

After "J.B.'s" death, Vera, his secretary-wife, and a long-time friend, the Rev. Edwin Robertson (collaborator on some of his translation work), brought to my favourite bookshop, and thence to my shelves, a slender paperback, *The Wounded Healer*, in which they told of his ministry through books. Countless people wrote to him – some, not slow to confess a problem with the translation of Matthew 5:48, the Authorized Version being a case in point: "Be ye therefore perfect, even as your Father which is in heaven is perfect." Admitting his own concern, J.B. Phillips had no translation of his own on the text, and after long labour – and honest as always – wrote how he "*clearly preferred the 'New English Bible' reading: 'You must therefore be all goodness just as your Heavenly Father is all good'.*" One cannot go past that!

Prayers to mingle with my own

O God, when our use of this world is over and we make room for others, may we not leave anything ravished by our greed, or spoiled by our ignorance, but may we hand on our common heritage fairer and sweeter through our use of it. AMEN. (*Dr Walter Rauschenbusch*)

Many, up through the centuries, have prayed, one by one, using helpfully John Wesley's words:

O Thou who camest from above
　　The pure celestial fire to impart,
Kindle a flame of sacred love
　　On the mean altar of my heart!

There let it for Thy glory burn
　　With inextinguishable blaze;
And trembling to its source return,
　　In humble prayer and fervent praise.

Morning

O God, open my heart, I pray, as I open my eyes. Make

me ready to face this day that Thou hast given me:

Thou hast set my comings and goings amid the marvels of this great universe. I follow good men and women who, from age to age, have hushed their hearts, and bowed their heads to worship Thee.

Upon me, as upon them, the sun has risen, and set: and round about us all, continually, the seasons have waxed and waned – with colours, and scents, and sounds. And Thy gracious providence has supplied our daily needs.

Gracious God, everywhere present, I bless Thee, above all, for what I know of Thine inmost nature, through Jesus Christ. I bless Thee for the gospels, making known to us, His birth and childhood, His steady, compassionate ministry, His teaching, His death, and glorious rising again!

In His promised presence, to this hour, we go upon our way – with faith, and lasting wonder. AMEN.

Evening

Gracious Father, I am glad that I need never pretend during prayer.

> I am tired now, and my words do not come easily;
> And I have not kept all my bright promises of the morning;
> But Thy loving care, I know, continues unchanged.
> For this, I bless Thee. AMEN.

FIDELITY

The Harvest of the Spirit is Fidelity

In our busy, bustling days, it seems that many beautiful English words get dropped from daily use. And "fidelity", I fear, is one of them. Yet it's a quality without which life loses an essential that holds it together. It has its place, in that rich "harvest" verse in Galatians, with which we are both greeting each new day just now and gathering up our thanks at day's end.

Many of us might here find ourselves guessing at its meaning, since we have never been called to use it in daily conversation. When I find myself in that plight these days, I turn immediately to my large gift volume of *Collins English Dictionary*. It is seldom that I seek there in vain for a word I have failed to find in older, smaller volumes that I have grown up with, or, at best, find there only in a very stilted form. And in the very nature of "fidelity", that is insufficient – it is such a warm-hearted, caring word, close to life.

"Fidelity", Collins' definition says, is "devotion to duties, obligations" (then it grows more personal) "Loyalty or devotion, as to a person or cause; faithfulness to one's spouse, lover, etc." And I accept the right to include within this "etc", "fellow workman" – and then move on admiringly to share a fine example, if a more dramatic one than is often the case.

A steady reading of one's daily newspaper, favourite magazines, and a welcome acceptance of modern biographies, will occasionally bring out unknown, treasured examples of fidelity. My heartening story, at this moment, represents a saving reality in the life of Sir James Thornhill, when he was re-painting the interior of the dome of St Paul's. It was, of course, as any one of us can understand, having paused, even a moment or two, to look up under that great dome, a hazardous undertaking.

Things seemed to be going well enough. After some time, Sir James reached a point when he needed to pause, to appraise a figure he had painted. He had some doubt about its proportions – and rapt in artistic contemplation, he stepped back, bending his head this way and that – to check what he had done – right back to the very edge of the scaffolding!

One further step must have spelled a breathless drop in space, to the marble floor below. But he was spared it, by the natural, instant reaction of his fellow workman's fidelity – a well-established attitude when there was no time to consider what he should do. Had he called "Beware!" it could have worsened things. What he did, was plunge a large brush into a can of colour, and hurl it, splashing, onto the painting! It did not save it – but more importantly, it saved the painter, who, alarmed, leapt forward to save his previous work. It was all thanks to the established spirit of his fellow workman, for there was no time to think it out: it all depended on an established relationship of caring. And that's how "fidelity" operates in this life, at times!

It's "the harvest of the Spirit". Rather an attitude accepted, mounting up through time, proving sufficient in an unforeseen crisis. Its name is "Fidelity". We need to bring it out of the dictionary, and *lodge it lovingly, vitally, at the heart of our human relationships*!

We do not often use the word these days, much less do we speak of "the integrity of God", "the integrity of Christ, our Lord". *Why not*?

Is it that we use more words to say the same thing – to glory in the same indispensable relationship?

* * *

God – approaching us each, in Christ – asks us, using the words of the beloved Dr George Matheson:

> Couldst thou love Me
> When creeds are breaking
> Old landmarks shaking . . .
> And rest thy heart *on Me*?

"Blessed is he, she," I say, "who can respond with the glorious consent of every faculty: 'YES! YES! YES! IN THE NAME OF JESUS CHRIST! YES!'"

* * *

> This, this is the God we adore,
>   Our faithful, unchangeable Friend;
> Whose love is as great as His power,
>   And neither knows measure nor end.

> 'Tis Jesus, the first and the last.
>   Whose Spirit shall guide us safe home;
> We'll praise Him for all that is past,
>   And trust Him for all that's to come.
>   (Joseph Hart,
>   in *The Methodist Hymn Book*)

To read, and rejoice in, later

New Testament

It surprised me that the word **Fidelity** is not to be found more than once in my Authorized Version of the Bible – skipping the Old Testament altogether. It appears only in "The Epistle of Paul to Titus" (chapter 2:9-10). "And who", you may well ask, "was Titus? Was he a servant, or a master of servants, that Paul used the word he chose, and which comes to us translated as *Fidelity*?"

I have never till lately sought out the answer to that question, and I had no handy ministerial friend, to whom I could address it. So I took down, from one of my study shelves, Dr James Hastings' mighty tome, which I seldom handle, so heavy is it: *Dictionary of the Bible*. But there awaited me an exact answer: "Titus", he took pleasure in believing, "was a convert from heathenism, probably won by St Paul himself." (And he referred me to Galatians 2:3.) Later on, I found Paul addressing Titus very affectionately as "To Titus, mine own son after the common faith" (Titus 1:4). "Neither his age, nor his place of birth is told us", says Dr Hastings. "We meet him first", he goes on to say, "when he accompanies St Paul on a journey from Antioch to Jerusalem."

Here and there, later, we catch fleeting references to Titus and his Christian service, again and again as a bearer of letters from Paul himself to scattered gatherings of the Church. And a wonderfully warm welcome they got, in that long ago time, arriving quite unexpectedly, when there was no *organized* letter delivery anywhere. Such a treasured link, depended – as in the case of Titus – on other Christians going by a certain route and being, in each case, *persons of unquestioned fidelity*.

This valued service that Titus rendered – though then often dangerous – may seem to us, now, "ordinary enough", but in those times, it took rare Christian spirit. Titus – as well as Paul – would have agreed, as a matter of unquestioned fact, with poet Robert Browning, much nearer our own time:

> Religion's all or nothing; it's no mere smile
> O' contentment, sigh of aspiration, sir –
> .... *rather stuff*
> *O' the very stuff, life of life, and self of self.*

Paul used the word meaning "*Fidelity*" for it – and Luther, in his turn, introduced that lovely understanding into his own home-life. Of his dear Katie, he wrote: "When I look at all the women in the world, I find none of whom I could boast as I boast with joyful conscience of my own. This one God Himself gave to me, and I know that He and all the angels are pleased when I hold fast to her in love and *fidelity*."

To ponder in our Modern World

To Titus, in his ministry, Paul wrote very down-to-earth injunctions (See Titus, chapter 2:1-10).

> "Speak thou the things which become sound doctrine: that the aged men be sober, grave, temperate, sound in faith, in charity, in patience. The aged women likewise, that they be in behaviour as becometh holiness, not false accusers, not given to much wine, teachers of good things; that they may teach the young women to be sober, to love their husbands, to love their children, to be discreet, chaste, keepers at home, good, obedient to their own husbands, that the word of God be not blasphemed. Young men likewise exhort to be sober

minded. In all things shewing thyself a pattern of good works; in doctrine showing uncorruptness, gravity, sincerity, sound speech, that cannot be condemned; that he that is of the contrary part may be ashamed, having no evil thing to say of you. Exhort servants to be obedient unto their own masters, and to please them well in all things; not answering again; not purloining, but *shewing all good fidelity*; that they may adorn the doctrine of God our Saviour in all things."

It sounds quaint in many ways to our modern ears, but it all adds up to overall "fidelity" – and we know what that means, though the word itself is seldom or never on a preacher's lips these days. (He now uses many more words to say as much.)

*

The Apocrypha uses the word "fidelity" once – but these days Christians seldom turn its pages, for "The Book of Esther" is less known even than "The Epistle of Paul to Titus".

*

To the Celt each new day is a gift, a flower, above all, a mystery which calls for the companionship of God if a man would see it well through. Hence the old prayer: "God be with me in this. Thy day, every day and every way, with me and for me, in this Thy day."

(*Hebridean Altars*)

*

Day after day –

"The new life begins now, right here in the midst of this changing and transient world." (*John La Farge*)

*

Something is happening around me; the dark is less dark, the silence is less deep. Even the air is changing. It is damper, sweeter. Morning is at hand. Light will soon come flooding over the edge of the world . . . What a gift!

(Anon)

GENTLENESS

The Harvest of the Spirit is Gentleness

The day I made ready to leave my friends a little way out of our beautiful southern city of Christchurch, they asked a favour of me, which was in fact no favour at all. Would I go and visit a long-time friend of theirs in a little railway town as I passed through? I gladly undertook to do that – the more readily when I learned that she *lived alone*, in a *flower-blessed garden*, and *was a great book lover*!

"You'll be Miss Snowden?" were her first words, as she greeted me with a smile. And with that, she snatched off her raffish old straw hat. "Come inside", were her next words, "and see my Polar pictures." And with that, we crossed over her doorstep.

I was charmed at once with the room that opened to my gaze, showing lots of books, a fine piano, pieces of pottery, and all down one wall, the pictures I had learned she possessed! They were beautiful, sensitive paintings of the Antarctic by Dr Edward Wilson who, sharing a hazardous expedition with Captain Scott, died along with him, in a little tent set in the great snowy spaces. I myself had two lovely books about him, carrying reproductions of a number of his paintings. *But these were originals*!

"How did you come by these? – they're beautiful." "I got them as a gift", said she, "from Mrs Wilson, when I kept her company in London, whilst he was away – and she delighted to offer them, for the little home I was setting up."

Then we started to read aloud to each other in turn, from her copies of two books I also possessed and loved, written by George Seaver. And I handled the tiny Union

Jack that Dr Wilson had carried to the Pole for her, and which was returned, after his death, to be set up in a place of honour above her mantel-piece, along with an envelope carrying a message from Captain Scott, and a card she equally treasured.

I opened her copy of a book at hand, and read aloud my favourite passage. "Now," – taking it from me, she said, "let me read you one of mine." It was plain we both had many more than one, though we both liked especially, how, on the journey south, he regularly climbed up into the silence of The Crow's Nest on their old ship, to keep a period of Devotions at an appointed time, as arranged with his wife away back in London. Only after his death, was this spiritual secret shared with the world, through their published letters. "My private chapel" he called it.

"Yes," said his understanding friend, now at my elbow, "he was a fine gentleman – yes, a very fine gentleman!"

So time passed; and she played to me, on her piano. Then, suddenly remembering the time, and glancing at the clock, said she, "I must make you a cup of tea!"

"Oh, don't bother", I replied, as she rose, "go out again into your garden, while the sun lasts."

"Look!" said she, *"we'll just have it in the nude, on the end of the kitchen-bench"* – which meant that we shared it without benefit of the best cloth, best cups and silver teapot: Such was the spirit engendered between us!

That night, she came to my lecture in the little town. "I hope you didn't think me an 'old duffer' this afternoon," she said, "but I had a lovely time. I so seldom, these days, meet anyone who knows and loves these people I love!"

As for myself, I was already counting it one of the most rewarding afternoons in my months of travel! Strength, and *gentleness* are not, in this world, that common – for all that neither of us needed a dictionary to offer us a definition.

A brief time I spent in India, will always remind me of a beautiful companion character – to balance out the sexes and a freezing place with a stifling hot one – long after I ceased mingling with the surging crowds about me. Now I was thinking of the ministry of Edwina Mountbatten, that lovely, very gentle person, during the time she shared India's crowds, grandeur, poverty and heat with her distinguished husband.

As their departure drew near, they were tendered a State banquet. It was a glittering occasion, a Cabinet occasion. Pandit Nehru paid his tribute, which was reported in newspapers the world round. Especially do I treasure what he said to Edwina: "The gods, or some good fairy, gave you beauty and high intelligence, and grace and charm and vitality – great gifts – and she who possesses them is a great lady wherever she goes. But unto those who have, even more shall be given: and they gave you something that was even rarer: the human touch, the love of humanity, the urge to serve those who suffer and who are in distress. . . . Is it surprising, therefore, that the people of India should love you, and look up to you as one of themselves? And now grieve that you are going?"

No, we do not need a dictionary to define "gentleness" – it speaks for itself. *It is always a blessed gift in a needy world*!

To read and ponder

Those many who knew Saul, the aggressor, when he hounded the early followers of Christ, and struck fear into all hearts, must have marvelled at the change in his spirit, following on his sudden, and surprising, experience on the Damascus Road!

Who among them would ever dream that a day would

come when as Paul, the loyal lover of Christ, he would be sending off a letter to the young helper Timothy? – a letter that would be read by Christians, the world round, all these centuries later!

Yet, so it is. For this very day, and not for the first time, I pause a moment to read words I find in that letter: "The Lord's servant must not be quarrelsome, but kindly to every one, an apt teacher, forbearing, correcting his opponents *with gentleness*" (The Second Letter of Paul to Timothy 2:25, R.S.V.).

*

You and I speaking English, need no definition of this lovely, luminous, warm, living, supportive word. No word in our language, or in our living day by day, comes closer to life! It is a truly Christian word!

*

And at no time, since our newspapers – reporting national, home, business and community life – have commanded our daily attention, have we so noticed its absence from the vocabulary and spirit of our general concerns. The word "violence" is more often in the world's headlines. And this is an urgent challenge to all followers of Christ – wherever life finds us.

Upon the very first pages in our New Testament, are these words: "*How blest are those of a gentle spirit*; they shall have the earth for their possession" (Matthew 5:5, New English Bible).

How long must we wait – and pray – and serve, before this becomes a popular conviction?

Daily I would pray:

> God be in my head:
>   And in my understanding;
> God be in mine eyes:
>   And in my looking;

God be in my mouth:
   And in my speaking;
God be in my heart:
   And in my thinking;
God be at mine end:
   And at my departing.

(From *A Sarum Primer*, 1558)

Prayers

Morning

Gracious God, in this great world of extremes there are lonely places; and teeming, surging crowds of needy, numberless people. And in between, places like our own – where it is easy to forget how much *gentleness* counts. If life is to be good, we constantly seek this precious gift of Thy Spirit.

Deliver us, we pray Thee, from self-importance, and haste; from carelessness and common thoughtlessness. Let the Spirit of Christ dwell in our hearts, with His gracious awareness, as we go about amongst others.

Grant especially, *wisdom and gentleness*, to all who order the affairs of nations; to all who command forces of trained power, that threaten peace in our world. Grant Thy grace to those dealing with ordinary people; and in so many parts of the suffering world, milling masses of refugees. Let gentleness never be scorned, forgotten, or even undervalued in human affairs. And let us take time enough, where we are at this moment, to offer what we have, that it may help.

Scatter the secret designs of all set on violence, I pray. Let peace be established in our homes, communities and countries. Give us, as a people, endless patience.

Establish, beyond question, lasting spiritual values. And in Thy mercy, support all men and women amongst us who, year in, year out, seek Thy peace and pursue it. In the Living Name of Christ, our Lord. AMEN.

Evening

From time to time, beyond human remembrance, men and women like us have hushed their hearts at day's end, to seek Thy lasting forgiveness, and to offer Thee praise, for Thine outpouring Love.

I bless Thee for my home, where loyalty and love dwell; where important values are shared, where laughter and joy have a natural place. I bless Thee for books, and music, and good conversation. I rejoice in "the comings and goings" of our working days; and for the strong, supportive experience of worship, at each week's beginning.

Let no disappointment of yesterday hold us back from joyous and meaningful service today; no involvement in our own plans find us unconcerned with the ongoing lives of others. I rejoice that around me are very many more good men and women than evil, despite the reports of newspaper headlines; many more men and women of ready helpfulness, than those of evil, selfish intent. Bless especially, I pray, any who serve Thy Church, in this great world. AMEN.

Prayers
To nourish my spirit in the Quiet Place

Morning

Almighty God, our Father Eternal, Thou hast fashioned our faltering hearts to seek Thee, and to know Thy Love.

I come, with no merits of my own, but with wonder and

expectation, through Jesus Christ, Thy Son, my Saviour.

I give thanks for safe-keeping through the night; and for another day. Let me not require of any about me this day, any higher standard of behaviour than I require of myself.

Let me be as ready to forgive another, as I am to accept forgiveness for myself. Enable me to walk humbly this day, with sincerity in my service, and joyful devotion.

Keep my mind and heart open, I pray Thee, to the acceptance of new truths; ever faithful to what I already know. Let my loving concern for Thy Kingdom in the hearts of men and women, begin here – and now.

Let me rejoice this day with those who do rejoice, and show pity to those who suffer, are lonely, or lack courage to go on.

Where there is domination, let me bring Christ's sweet gift of mercy; where there is friction, let me offer the gentle gift of respect; where there is no sense of direction, let me glory in the assurance that Christ is The Way.
AMEN.

Evening

Grant me Thy Peace and Serenity, I pray Thee, O God, as I look back over this day, and I lie down to sleep.

If I have not seen the outcome of my service this day, give me patience, and a lively expectation on the morrow.

Gather this night, into Thy holy keeping, any I know of who are in fear, in deep anxiety, in loneliness. I name them in Thy Loving presence ——————

Keep me mindful always, as I come to sum up my day, that people matter more than things.

Bless and keep this night, I pray especially, the head-strong and the foolish; the careless and the ignorant. Support the innocent and the inexperienced. Thou knowest – as no one about us does – their hidden needs. And Thou art ever able to meet them.

Forgive me, if ever I have felt a little superior, ready to smile at others' poor efforts. Forgive me, that often my response to Thee is poor too.

Grant me Thy gift of peace, as sleep comes now. For Christ's sake. AMEN.

SELF-CONTROL

The Harvest of the Spirit is Self-Control

At the very dawn of Time, a young man had trouble with lack of self-control. His name was Cain. His brother, Abel, was a keeper of sheep, whilst he himself was a tiller of the soil. (This we are told in the early pages of the Bible, in Genesis 4:1-2.) Unhappily, it's a story not yet out of date. One has only to look at the police court headlines in most of our daily newspapers.

Modern-day poet, Karen Gershon reminds us:

> Cain was the first-born, cast
> from the breast to the bracken and the brook
> and a wild landscape of secluded days.
>
> The hillside set horizons to his thoughts.
> His life stretched acres: strong and fruitful ground.
> Time fell in trees: an eye cut into the forest.
>
> Abel had many voices. Cain
> had the green voice of water and the wind
> to finger the labour of his seeds.
>
> He was the weather's harbour in the hills,
> the seasons hung like jesses on his heels,
> and when the god showed him his servitude
>
> the landscape ploughed its talons through his mood,
> gathering his many bitter years
> into a terror to torment his blood.

From his tilled soil Cain brought a sacrifice of his fruits, when the time was ripe. But brother Abel's offering from his flock was more acceptable. *And lacking self-control, in a terrible all-consuming rush of passion, Cain killed his brother.*

"To us", as Dr William Barclay, my friend, said, "it seems quite arbitrary . . . little reason or justice in the story. The meaning may well be that the only offering which a man can bring to God (in the thinking of the Hebrews) *is the most precious thing* . . . Now the most precious thing that life supplies is life itself . . . If that principle be accepted, then the only true sacrifice to God, in those primitive days, was a sacrifice of blood."

A moment's lack of self-control, his arm raised – and what Cain did may have shocked him greatly, when his brother, smitten, failed to rise from the ground, since it was his grim harvest to be the first passionate man ever to face the fact of Death.

* * *

Let me share an experience that brought to me a wonderful strength in a consideration of men and women of these times, who have shown great self-control. I was in London, and found my way to a little sacred spot, called Postman's Park.

It is hedged around by great buildings – the G.P.O. among others – and is not generally known to tourists, more's the pity. (I've never met anyone who has talked about it except my friend Frank, and it's one of my best "finds".) It sprang out of the heart and mind of the famous painter, G.F. Watts, and was realized through the friendly aid of the Vicar of St Botolph's Aldersgate, London.

Central in the little park is an arcade with seats, and running from end to end are fifty-three memorial tiles, bearing a tribute to men and women, boys and girls, who in their ordinary life, *showed remarkable self-control*. The very youngest was little Harry Bristow, of Walthamstowe, aged eight, "who saved his little sister's life, on 30th December 1890, by tearing off her flaming clothes, but caught fire himself, and died of burns and shock".

And my heart was strangely moved to see how many trades and occupations were represented. Ernest Benning, was a young "compositor, aged twenty-two, who, upset from a boat one dark night off Pimlico Pier, grasped an oar with one hand, supporting a woman with the other, but sank as she was rescued". "Walter Peart, driver, and Harry Dean, fireman of the Windsor Express, on 18th July 1858, whilst scalded and burnt, sacrificed their lives – but saved the train."

And "Mary Rogers, stewardess of the *Stella*, gave up her life-belt, and with it her life, during an Easter Channel crossing." And there was the self-control of Greenhoff, "who died in a terrible explosion at Silverstown, in January 1917". He might have saved himself, except that "by sticking to his post, he saved many others". Nor must I forget "William Freer Lucas, M.R.C.S., L.L.D., of Middlesex Hospital, who risked poison for himself rather than lessen the chance of saving a child's life". Many women were recorded, young and old, mothers, housewives, grannies, a pantomime artist, a daughter of a brick-layer's labourer. They were all so much of the pattern of self-control in everyday life, that there was nothing of weakness nor unworthy sentimentality present.

(It was all so natural – with people taking their lunch seated about me here and there on the seats provided, and little sparrows, just as naturally, hopping about, picking up the crumbs that dropped.)

Prayers to mingle with my own

Morning

O God, our Living, Loving Father, unhindered by the limitations that we, Thy children, know, let us move into this new day, with a glad sense of Thy gracious presence.

We are not wise enough, loving, or strong enough to journey alone. But Thy Fatherly concern for us each, never falters, never fails. And with that confidence, we go out into this new day.

Fascinated by the beauty of the earth and sky; and by the fertility of grass, and gardens, we move out to meet the many other signs of Thy presence. And in life's secret places, where no signs are, we yet trust Thee, with our response.

Thou hast shown us the unquestionable Love, and Life and endless Values of Jesus Christ, our Lord. And we put our day-to-day Faith in Him. We find closeness and victory, again and again, in His sustaining Power.

Enable us, in any experience of tension, to show self-control, as the outcome of His support; to face fresh situations without fear; to be sensible of others' needs as we mingle with them outside our home today.

Bless those of us who bear constant burdens of responsibility – needing to make far-reaching judgements that affect others; called upon to instruct and direct others, as yet inexperienced; offering encouragement and companionship to any others about us who stand in special need of these gifts and graces today. And enable us to walk humbly, and yet joyfully, on our way. AMEN.

*

Help me, O God, to meet in the right way, and in the right spirit, everything which comes to me today.

Help me to approach my work cheerfully, and my tasks diligently.

Help me to meet people courteously and, if need be, to suffer fools gladly.

*

Gracious Father, from this place, so familiar at this hour of the day, I bring Thee praise for Thy continuing mercies. I give Thee thanks in particular for refreshment of body, mind and spirit.

Forgive me that I have ever taken upon my lips complimentary words, without fully knowing their rich content. The word "self-control" is one such. It is so easy to overlook its spiritual content, and thus refer to it too lightly.

Forgive me, and enable me to glory in those occasions when I can happily use it of a personality in our day, in our midst.

Of so many of my fellow earth dwellers I am afraid to claim too much. Liberate me from that approach, I pray Thee, and let me rejoice in every sign of self-control.

I bless Thee, above all, for what I know of *the character of Jesus Christ*. In all manner of circumstances, I see that lovely spiritual quality shining through.

I rejoice in what the Gospel records have revealed of His countless human relationships. I am glad to be told of His birth in Bethlehem; His natural growing up in Nazareth, part of a humble, but honourable family. I rejoice in His service as a village carpenter, in the skills that resided in His hands. And for the loving respect He extended to men and women with whom He had dealings.

I rejoice especially that His call to serve Thy Divine purposes among faltering earth dwellers, found Him wholly responsive. For the early calling of His disciples, I bless Thee – and that His call still rings out to us upon life's shore.

For His teaching, His Cross, and His glorious rising

again; and for His lasting Presence, ever near, evermore. I would love, and follow Him faithfully. AMEN.

*

Help me to meet disappointments, frustrations, hindrances or opposition, calmly, and without irritation.

Help me to meet delays with patience, and unreasonable demands *with self-control* . . .

Keep me serene all through today. All this I ask for Jesu's sake. AMEN. (*Dr William Barclay*)

*

Lord, make me an instrument of Thy peace. Where there is hatred, let me sow love. Where there is injury, pardon. Where there is doubt, faith. Where there is despair, hope. Where there is darkness, light. Where there is sadness, joy.

*

O Divine Master, grant that I may not so much seek to be consoled, as to console; to be understood, as to understand; to be loved, as to love; for it is in giving that we receive, it is in pardoning that we are pardoned, and it is in dying that we are born to eternal life. (*St Francis of Assisi*)

*

Accompany me today, O Spirit Invisible, in all my goings, but stay with me also when I am in my own home, and among my kindred. Forbid that I should fail to show to those nearest to me the sympathy and consideration which Thy grace enables me to show to others with whom I have to do. Forbid that I should refuse to my own household the courtesy and politeness which I think proper to show to strangers. Let today begin at home.

Leave me not, O gracious Presence, in such hours as I may today devote to the reading of books or of newspapers. Guide my mind to choose the right books, and having chosen them, to read them in the right way. When I read for profit, grant that all I read may lead me nearer to Thyself. When I read for recreation, grant that what I read may not lead me away from Thee. Let all my reading so refresh my mind that I may the more eagerly seek after whatsoever things are pure and fair and true.

Let me have a special sense of Thy nearness to me, O God, in such times as I may be able to devote to prayer, to any public exercise of worship, or to the receiving of the Blessed Sacrament; through Jesus Christ my Lord. AMEN.

(*Dr John Baillie*)

Evening

Thou hast blessed my going out, this day; bless now my coming in, I pray Thee, O Lord God. I bless Thee, that I have no call to pretend in Thy presence, for Thou knowest me altogether.

Now, at the end of this day, I am tired – but I go to my sleep with utmost trust and abiding thankfulness.

Establish in my personality Thy gracious "goodness" – that I may waken to serve Thee more acceptably when the new day comes. For Christ's sake. AMEN.

*

As night closes about us like a soft garment, O God, grant me a renewed sense of Thy nearness. Forgive, I pray Thee, any foolish shortcoming or conscious sin that I have allowed into my life this day. Grant me, ere I sleep, not only Thy forgiveness – but such a vital sense of its reality, that when the new day comes, I may rise refreshed and strengthened, to go forth into Thy service unashamed, garrisoned with Hope and Joy.

Hold, too, in Thy Loving Care, this night and for ever, all whom I love; all whom I delight to know; all of whom I think, in thankfulness, just now . . . I name them before Thee, in this moment of hallowed Quietness. AMEN.

Dotting the blue are scudding clouds,
Over the clouds the sun,
Over the sun is *the Love of God*
Blessing us every one.

(Anon)

"As the Father hath loved Me", said our Lord and Master, "so have I loved you: *continue ye in My Love*" (John 15:9).

*

Let us put our Love, not into words or into talk, but into deeds, and make it real", says the New Testament letter-writer known as John the Elder, though he does not himself, in his writings, use that familiar name (1 John 3:18, Moffatt translation).

FESTIVAL DAYS!

Festival Days Unforgettable

Christmas

Readings and Prayers

And in that region there were shepherds out in the field, keeping watch over their flock by night. And an angel of the Lord appeared to them, and the glory of the Lord shone around them, and they were filled with fear. And the angel said to them, "Be not afraid: for behold, I bring you good news of a great joy which will come to all the people: for to you is born this day in the city of David a Saviour, who is Christ the Lord. And this will be a sign to you: you will find a babe wrapped in swaddling clothes and lying in a manger." And suddenly there was with the angel a multitude of the heavenly host praising God and saying,

> "Glory to God in the highest,
> and on earth, peace among men with whom he is
> pleased!"

When the angels went away from them into heaven, the shepherds said to one another, "Let us go over to Bethlehem and see this thing that has happened, which the Lord has made known to us." And they went with haste, and found Mary and Joseph, and the babe lying in a manger.

And when they saw it they made known the saying which had been told them concerning this child; and all who heard it wondered at what the shepherds told them.

But Mary kept all these things, pondering them in her heart (Luke 2:8-19. R.S.V.).

"BETHLEHEM OF JUDEA"

A little child,
   A shining star.
A stable rude,
   The door ajar.

Yet in that place,
   So rude, forlorn,
The Hope of all
   The world was born.

(Author Unknown)

We are none of us too poor, or stupid, or lowly – it was the simple shepherds who saw Him first. We are none of us too great, or learned, or rich – it was the three wise kings who came next and offered gifts. We are none of us too young . . . or too old. There is only one thing against most of us – we are too proud. (*Michael Fairless*)

No star in all the heights of heaven
But burned to see Him go;
Yet unto Earth alone was given
His human form to know.

(Unknown grateful heart)

Prayer

O God, this great world's greatest Surprise of all
   Time,
I rejoice in this Gift of Your Son – above all,
   Beloved.
Grant this reality may be central, in our Christmas-
   keeping, today.
Let no rich-tasting foods, and joyous songs, and
   bright baubles

wrest Him, ever, from His central place in our hearts
and lives.
Let our generous giving of carefully chosen gifts to
those we
closely love, in no wise take the place of the giving of
ourselves
to Christ, our Loving Saviour and Lord. Let His
Spirit live ever in
our hearts, and in all our doings
the whole year round, willingly,
joyously, I pray. AMEN.

Prayer

O perfect Love, outpassing sight,
O Light, beyond our ken,
Come down through all the world tonight
And heal the hearts of men!

(*Laurence Houseman*)

Prayer

O God, our Father, bless especially, this night, the sick,
and the frail, the lonely, the self-absorbed, the confused,
the discouraged.
Reveal the endless Wonder of Christmas to those who
do not know that Christ lives!

Thanksgiving

Because in tender majesty
Thou cam'st to earth, nor stayed till we,
Poor sinners, stumbled up to Thee,
I thank my God.

Because the Saviour of us all
Lay with the cattle in the stall,

121

Because the Great came to the small,
I thank my God.

(*G.A. Studdert-Kennedy*)

Festival Days

One there is no forgetting, is **New Year's Day**.

We men and women, as we grow in this Earth Life, often run out of ideas – but God never does! Every year that He gives us is, we find, A NEW YEAR. Despite the fact that it turns out to be of the same length, with the same number of seasons, in the same order – it reaches us with something wholly New! New ideas are given us, new friends, new undertakings we've never dreamed of before, new colleagues in service, new skills are found to reside in our hands, new hopes to quicken our travelling through the days. In actuality, we have not – any one of us – passed this way before. *This is a NEW YEAR!*

This love of newness is well established in Thy heart, O God! No one of us gets far into *his* New Testament, *her* New Testament, without being struck by Paul's rejoicing in this fact. In 2 Corinthians 5:6 we find Paul wrapped around by a splendid confidence: "*our sufficiency is of God*: Who hath made us all ministers of the *new testament*; not of the letter, but of the spirit: for the letter killeth, but the spirit giveth life."

And in the fifth chapter (2 Corinthians 5:17) he is saying, even more certainly: "*If any man be in Christ, he is a new creature* – old things are passed away; behold, *all things are become new*."

And I can't find any word of witness in biographies and autobiographies of the ongoing Christian centuries, to this day, more *graciously, more gladly used*!

The triumphant word picture of the End of Time finishes with the same assurance, and glory! "And I heard a great voice out of heaven saying, 'Behold, the tabernacle of God is with men, and He will dwell with them, and they shall be His people, and God himself shall be with them, and be their God.

"'And God shall wipe away all tears from their eyes; and there shall be no more death, neither sorrow, nor crying, neither shall there be any more pain: for the former things are passed away.' And He that sat upon the throne said, *Behold, I make all things new*'!" (Revelation 21:3-5)

* * *

The New Testament Challenge

"I appeal to you . . . by the mercies of God, to present your bodies as a living sacrifice, holy and acceptable to God, which is your spiritual worship. Do not be conformed to this world, but be transformed by the renewal of your mind, that you may prove what is the will of God, which is good and acceptable and perfect" (Romans 12:1, R.S.V.).

Prayer

Lord Jesus Christ, Son of the Living God,
teach us to walk in Your way more trustfully,
to accept Your truth more faithfully,
and to share Your life more lovingly.
By the power of the Holy Spirit
guide us in our work for the Church,
so that we may come as one family
to the Kingdom of the Father,
where You live for ever.
(National Pastoral Congress, Liverpool, 1980)

*

O God, Who hast bound us together in this bundle of life, give us grace to understand how our lives depend upon the courage, the industry, the honesty, and the integrity of our fellow men; that we may be mindful of their needs, grateful for their faithfulness, and faithful in our responsibilities to them; through Jesus Christ our Lord. AMEN. (*Dr Reinhold Niebuhr*, 1892-1971)

Evening Prayer

And now the day is done, O God, and the darkness gathers all living things in for rest;

And I seek for my rest of body, mind, and spirit, with those close to me, and sharing my needs.

From time beyond remembrance, others like me have hushed their hearts at the day's end.

Forgive me, I pray, for any unworthy word spoken this day, and for any unhelpful silence.

Take my shortsighted requests, and strip them of self-interest, give me courage to hold to Your long-time purposes;

Save me from vague goodwill that evades situations that seem difficult; and let my witness, where I live and work, be gracious.

Bless all whom I love and care about; and all who can make claims upon me in any way: —————— and —————— and —————— and —————————. AMEN.

The First Day of Lent

Not all Christians keep Lent, but to many of us it is a valuable period of forty week-days, from Ash Wednesday to Holy Saturday, commemorating our young Lord's fasting in the wilderness.

It does not come to us as "a lash for our spiritual laziness"; it comes to our minds and spirits as a helpful remembrance of His deep wholeness of devotion.

* * *

Prayers

O Thou Supreme! most secret and most present, most beautiful and strong! What shall I say, my God, my Life, my Holy Joy? What shall any man say when he speaks of Thee? (*St Augustine, 354-430*)

(And the same words are on my tongue – a Christian woman – all these centuries later.)

*

Grant to us, O Lord, to enter upon this holy fast with the armour of Christian warfare: that we who are to fight against spiritual wickedness, may be fortified by the power of self-denial. Through Christ, our Lord. (Ash Wednesday, Roman Missal)

Thanksgiving

Gracious God, I hush my heart in Your Presence this day, with great wonder. Year by year, I learn, as I go on living, what Lent really means. Guide me through its forty days, to an even richer spirit, I pray. Let me spell out in my ordinary life, a meaningful responsiveness, as I see it in the wilderness testing of Jesus.

Save me, O God, from slack indulgence; grant me a lively courage, and an ongoing eagerness. O God, I would put away all thoughtless words and cleverly contrived pretence – to speak the deepest desires of my heart. For Christ's sake. AMEN.

Evening Prayer

I bow my head to say that I am glad to have lived today – and to have come now to the day's end. I am fascinated by the fertility of the earth, by the beauty of mountains, and undulating countryside. The lakes and rivers mirror the skies, and the secret, lonely places challenge our resources. Today, I have learnt some things I never knew before; I have undertaken tasks that I have never tackled before. I have felt myself bound to others, in living obligations I have never been aware of before.

It has been a busy day – and with birds that fly homeward on tired wings, with creatures that gather their fellows about them, in safety, I seek my sleep thankfully.

Bring me, I pray, safely though the night, to the light of the new day – refreshed, and eager to do well what You require of me, in my setting. Forgive me, O God, if I have been impatient with anyone whom, later, I found to be doing his modest best. I bless You for all who have brought true service, and joy into the day. And may both go with us into the morrow. For Christ's sake. AMEN.

Good Friday

Few of us find it easy to discover since when, and

why, the Friday before Easter is called "Good Friday". Recalling what happened that day, most of us feel that the name given is anything but suitable, for so much that we can only call "bad" happened that day.

The first gospel in our New Testament says: Then the soldiers of the governor took Jesus into the praetorium, and they gathered the whole battalion before Him. And they stripped Him, and plaiting a crown of thorns they put it on His head, and put a reed in His right hand. And kneeling before Him, they mocked Him, saying, "Hail, King of the Jews!" And they spat upon Him, and they took the reed and struck Him on the head. And when they had mocked Him, they stripped Him of the robe, and put His own clothes on Him, and led Him away to crucify Him

(Matthew 27:27; R.S.V.).

* * *

And sitting down, they watched Him there,
The soldiers did;
There, while they played with dice,
He made His sacrifice,
And died upon the Cross to rid
God's world of sin.

(*G.A. Studdert-Kennedy*)

*

The word "Good Friday", authorities tell us, most likely arose, long afterwards from the term "God's Friday", counting the redemptive sacrifice of Christ's death, as indeed, the "good" thing it was, in dealing with man's sin. And so, it has remained, though in various sections of the

127

Church it is marked differently – in the Roman Church, with the altar and priests that day vested in black; a wooden clapper substituted for the little bell at the elevation of the host. In the Greek Church it is the fast that is very strictly kept. In the Lutheran Church the organ is silent. The Anglican Church, and some others, keep a three-hours service that day, consisting of Scripture readings, prayers, and a specific remembering of the "seven last words from the Cross".

Prayer

In private prayer, it is not easy, on this special morning, to gather my words, in this moment of quietness alone. They are coloured by all that I have read, and heard, of the hostile spirit of that crowd that condemned Jesus. I cannot forget the calm and strong dignity of their Prisoner, nor be unmindful of the cross-currents stirred by political and religious factions.

But I do not forget the bounds, and depths of Love – to this hour, an everlasting factor of that day, I celebrate. I am reassured by the faithfulness of the little band of followers who stood faithful, especially the women, though, like the men, bewildered and afraid.

I cannot but count "Good" on this day, our Saviour's prayer of Forgiveness for those who, like the rest of us, so often, know not what we do, when we pain His loving heart exceedingly. AMEN.

Prayer

No voice can sing, no heart can frame,
Nor can the memory find

128

A sweeter sound than Jesu's name,
 The Saviour of mankind.
O Hope of every contrite heart,
 O Joy of all the meek,
To those who ask how kind Thou art!
 How good to those who seek!
      (St Bernard of Clairvaux, 1091-1153)

Thanksgiving

The years pass, O Lord, the centuries pass – and much about us is changed; but I am reassured in the enduring presence and power of Christ, my Living, Forgiving Lord, Triumphant eternally.

Without Thee, I am as fickle as any long ago, caught up in the mood of the crowd; but in Thy holy keeping, I am safe.

Without Thee, my heart could hesitate, and be for ever afterwards grieved – like that of Judas. But with Thee, is safe-keeping, O Lord!

Again and again, like dear, impulsive Peter, would I know myself unreliable – but despite my human frailty, I do not face each day alone.

I may be as frightened of public opinion as Pilate – but I am not left to make important, far-reaching decisions alone.

And for these blessed, secret realities, I give fresh Thanks every Good Friday – for in very truth, these multiple realities make this day "Good".

         AMEN.

Easter Day

Readings:

Now in the place where He was crucified there was a garden; and in the garden a new sepulchre, wherein was never man yet laid. There laid they Jesus therefore because of the Jews' preparation day; for the sepulchre was nigh at hand. (John 19:41).

The first day of the week cometh Mary Magdalene early, when it was yet dark, unto the sepulchre, and seeth the stone rolled away from the sepulchre. Then she runneth, and cometh to Simon Peter, and to the other disciple, whom Jesus loved, and saith unto them, "They have taken away the Lord out of the sepulchre, and we know not where they have laid Him." (John 20:1-2).

Poem

When Mary thro' the garden went,
　　There was no sound of any bird,
And yet, because the night was spent,
　　The little grasses lightly stirred,
　　The flowers awoke, the lilies heard.

When Mary thro' the garden went,
　　The dew lay still on flower and grass,
The waving palms above her sent
　　Their fragrance out as she did pass,
　　No light upon the branches was.

When Mary thro' the garden went,
　　Her eyes, for weeping long, were dim,
The grass beneath her footsteps bent,

The solemn lilies, white and slim,
These also stood and wept for Him.

When Mary thro' the garden went,
  She sought, within the garden ground,
One for Whom her heart was rent,
  One Who for her sake was bound,
  One Who sought and she was found.

(*Mary R. Coleridge*)

(*Read on into John 20, picturing the scene*)

*

And many other signs truly did Jesus in the presence of His disciples, which are not written in this book: But these are written, that ye might believe that Jesus is the Christ, the Son of God; and that believing ye might have life through His name. (John 20:30-31)

Old Carol

But one, and one alone remained,
  With love that could not vary;
And thus a joy past joy she gained,
  That sometime sinner, Mary,
    Alleluya, Alleluya:
The first the dear, dear form to see
Of him that hung upon the tree:
    Hosanna in excelsis!

*

How wonderful is the first New Testament statement with which we found ourselves entering into our Easter rejoicing! "*Now in the place where He was crucified there was a garden*" – an everlasting reminder, world round, as Easter comes, is LIFE FROM APPARENT DEATH!

The only reality that reaches us more closely, is our Risen Lord's Own!

He doesn't argue about it! He merely states it as lasting Truth. Actually, it isn't much to say; **but coming from Him, it is all we, his followers, one by one, ever need to hear**: "*Because I live, ye shall live also*" (John 14:19).

My Easter Response

Gracious, Living Lord, I add my rejoicing to countless others the world round since that first surprising Easter morning – supported so soon by Paul, sending out his everlasting question to all following his loved, living Lord: "What shall separate us from the love of Christ? Shall . . . life, shall death? Nay!" (Romans 8:35-37).

*

I am no longer my own, but Thine.
Put me to what Thou wilt, rank me with whom Thou wilt:
Put me to doing: put me to suffering:
Let me be employed for Thee, or laid aside for Thee:
Exalted for Thee, or brought low for Thee:
Let me be full, let me be empty:
Let me have all things: let me have nothing:
I freely and heartily yield all things to Thy pleasure and disposal.
And now, O glorious and blessed God, Father, Son and Holy Spirit,
Thou art mine, and I am Thine. So be it.
And the covenant which I have made on earth, let it be ratified in heaven.

(Methodist Covenant Service)

Whitsunday

It has never been easy to put some realities into "earth-words". Dr Ralph Sockman, the distinguished radio messenger, is right: "The Holy Spirit is better apprehended *in action* than in definition." True! So is the Wind! "The top of the hill is my favourite place", said a youthful companion to me once, as we started to climb, "because the-air-in-a-hurry there is so fresh. I like it!"

"Air-in-a-hurry" seemed a good name for the exhilaration we shared. That's the secret of the wind – it drives away stuffiness, lifelessness, smugness.

No one of us can really live without an experience of the wind. Certainly, Jesus loved the wind. As a youth, I can visualize Him racing with friends up on the friendly nearby Nazareth hills, the wind in His hair!

And He had not long started His ministry, when He was questioned deeply, as He sat with Nicodemus, a Pharisee and member of the Sanhedrin, in the cool of the evening on the flat rooftop. There, the wind lightly touched His face and garments (John 3:8).

Later, when His Christian Church was brought into the world, *it was born in a wind*. (The book of The Acts of the Apostles attempts to set it down in words, although words are so limited: "When the day of Pentecost was fully come, they" – the early followers of Jesus – "were all with one accord in one place. And suddenly there came a sound from heaven as of *a mighty rushing wind*" (Acts 2:1-2). *And in that gift, came exhilaration, liveliness, gladness!* Dullness, selfishness, casualness were done away!

*

Becoming a Christian, to this day, isn't just joining a congregation – it's a new experience of LIFE! "Always there are unmistakable signs when the power of the Spirit goes to work", says my honoured and beloved Scottish friend, Dr J.S. Stewart, in his book, *The Wind of the*

Spirit. "When a man once weak and shifty and unreliable becomes strong and clean and victorious; when a church once stagnant and conventional and introverted throws off its dull tedium and catches fire and becomes alert and missionary-minded; when Christians of different denominations begin to realize there is far more in the Risen Christ to unite them than there can be anywhere to divide them – then, the world is made to know that something is happening."

Prayers

> O thou who camest from above,
> The pure celestial fire to impart,
> Kindle a flame of sacred Love
> On the mean altar of my heart.

(*Charles Wesley*)

*

O Lord, Who hast taught us that all our doings, without love, are nothing worth; send Thy Holy Spirit, and pour into our hearts that most excellent gift of love, the very bond of peace, and of all virtues, without which whosoever liveth is counted dead before Thee; Grant this for Thine only Son Jesus Christ's sake. AMEN.

(Book of Common Prayer)

*

O God, we thank Thee for the sweet refreshment of sleep, and for the glory and vigour of the new day. As we set our faces once more toward our daily work, we pray thee for the strength sufficient for our tasks. May Christ's spirit of duty and service ennoble all we do. Uphold us by the consciousness that our work is useful work, and a blessing to all.

If there has been anything in our work harmful to others, and dishonourable to ourselves, reveal it to our inner eye with such clearness that we shall hate it, and put it away, though it be at a loss to ourselves.

When we work with others, help us to regard them, not as servants to our will, but as being equal to us in human dignity, and equally worthy of their full reward.

May there be nothing in this day's work of which we shall be ashamed when the sun is set, nor in the eventide of our life when our task is done . . . and we meet Thy face. AMEN. (*Dr Walter Rauschenbusch*)

Prayers

Morning

Ever Loving God, I waken with immediate thanks for safe-keeping through the night.

I rejoice in my earth-family relationships, and in the love of countless others who have enriched me through the years. Save me, I pray, from ever taking these gracious things for granted.

Quicken my capacity to love Thee today, and to love all with whom I share its hours of work and leisure. Especially do I pray for those who can find no work to do – despite all their seeking.

I rejoice in the light, and warmth of the sun, constant in its rising; and in the cheerful colours of grass and gardens. I respond with surprise to many new experiences, as they come.

I marvel at the trustfulness of animal pets; and the lively plumage and songs of birds. I give Thee thanks for great trees, with their tall shapes against the skies, and for their welcoming shade.

I sense anew Thy greatness, and supporting strength, before Thy massive mountains, and hills up-raised. I give thanks for the quietness that awaits us there – and the ever challenging sense of perspective in this life.

Our need is to know, deeply, continually and sincerely, that people matter more than property; that the experience of giving often outmatches the joy of receiving.

So would I live, in the Service and Spirit of Jesus, our Lord. AMEN.

Evening

Gracious Father, Thou hast blessed me this day, in my going out, bless me now in my coming in, I pray. From time beyond remembrance, men and women have hushed their hearts in Thy presence at the day's end, and I do that now.

Here, shedding all pretence, I voice my inmost thoughts, with utmost honesty; here, I pause to give thanks for the richest experiences of my life; and I pray that I may be continally aware of Thy presence, in service.

I commit to Thy keeping, all dear to me, far and near, young and old. Bless the energy, and continuing good judgement of all whose work is lonely; all whose retirement seems long in coming; all whose monetary reward seems modest.

So, in this quietness, let me sort out my priorities, before I give myself to sleep. In the Name of Christ, *Look, Father, look on His anointed face, And only look on us as found in Him*. AMEN.

*

And a final prayer from my friend in writing, Elsie Parry:

> *Take my failure, Lord,*
> *All I have tried to do,*
> *All I have longed to be,*
> *Yet not attained.*
> *These, the unfulfilled,*
> *I bring to You.*

BOOKS BY RITA SNOWDEN

Continually Aware

Here Rita Snowden affirms her faith and shows how familiar Bible verses – and more mundane things in life – can take on fresh meaning if we are only continually aware in our approach to them.

Good Company

Rita Snowden invites us to spend time in the company of St Luke and enjoy the warmth of his gospel which meets the needs of our ordinary lives in the twentieth century.

Like Wind on the Grasses

Touching on her own memories, on the joys and sorrows around us and returning always to the events and message of the Gospel, here is a belief that we can share and a book that is as wide ranging as the wind itself.

Prayers In Large Print

"For the many with failing sight in the autumn tide of life, this little volume will be a blessing . . .

Methodist Recorder

Secrets

Rita Snowden shows the more poetic side of her thinking in this book of poems which she has written over the years, and which mean a great deal to her.

Also available in Fount Paperbacks

BOOKS BY WILLIAM BARCLAY

Jesus of Nazareth

'The book is in Dr Barclay's usual readable and straightforward style and is quite worthy of the film, as the film was of the book.'
Life and Work

In the Hands of God
Ed. BY RITA SNOWDEN

William Barclay's *British Weekly* articles have brought comfort, understanding and pleasure to thousands. These articles help us to take a fresh look at our own lives and the people in them.

Prayers for Young People

Morning and evening prayers for every week of the year, designed to help young people to pray, and with a fine introductory chapter on 'You and Your Prayers'.

More Prayers for Young People

'William Barclay has provided excellent help . . . All Dr Barclay's well-known virtues of clarity and soundness are present.'
Church Times

The Plain Man Looks at the Apostles' Creed

'An excellent book for a serious-minded Church study group . . . It would also provide . . . the right material for a series of talks on the Apostles' Creed. Once again Professor Barclay has done a great service for his fellow Christians in the Church.'
Expository Times

Also available in Fount Paperbacks

The Mind of St Paul
WILLIAM BARCLAY

'There is a deceptive simplicity about this fine exposition of Pauline thought at once popular and deeply theological. The Hebrew and Greek backgrounds are described and all the main themes are lightly but fully treated.'   *The Yorkshire Post*

The Plain Man Looks at the Beatitudes
WILLIAM BARCLAY

'. . . the author's easy style should render it . . . valuable and acceptable to the ordinary reader.'   *Church Times*

The Plain Man Looks at the Lord's Prayer
WILLIAM BARCLAY

Professor Barclay shows how this prayer that Jesus gave to his disciples is at once a summary of Christian teaching and a pattern for all prayers.

The Plain Man's Guide to Ethics
WILLIAM BARCLAY

The author demonstrates beyond all possible doubt that the Ten Commandments are the most relevant document in the world today and are totally related to mankind's capacity to live and make sense of it all within a Christian context.

Ethics in a Permissive Society
WILLIAM BARCLAY

How do we as Christians deal with such problems as drug taking, the 'pill', alcohol, morality of all kinds, in a society whose members are often ignorant of the Church's teaching? Professor Barclay approaches a difficult and vexed question with his usual humanity and clarity, asking what Christ himself would say or do in our world today.

The Perfection of Love
Tony Castle

The great spiritual masters have a message for us today. This is a collection of passages from their writing, drawn from all the traditions of Christianity.

I Am With You
John Woolley

Drawn together by one who works among the seriously ill, this book contains prayers which will bring comfort and help to the troubled.

Moments With God
Georgette Butcher

A collection of prayers and readings specially designed for women. The author shows how God can help and guide us through the changing pattern of each day.

Yes, Lord, I Believe
Dom Edmund Jones

". . . a very positive and practical book . . . a helpful source of prayer. The freshness, honesty and vitality of its style ensure that its message is deeply and immediately felt."

The Universe

Also available in Fount Paperbacks

Fount Paperbacks

Fount is one of the leading paperback publishers of religious books and below are some of its recent titles.

- [ ] GETHSEMANE Martin Israel £2.50
- [ ] HIS HEALING TOUCH Michael Buckley £2.50
- [ ] YES TO LIFE David Clarke £2.95
- [ ] THE DIVORCED CATHOLIC Edmund Flood £1.95
- [ ] THE WORLD WALKS BY Sue Masham £2.95
- [ ] C. S. LEWIS: THE MAN AND HIS GOD
      Richard Harries £1.75
- [ ] BEING FRIENDS Peter Levin £2.95
- [ ] DON'T BE AFRAID TO SAY YOU'RE LONELY
      Christopher Martin £2.50
- [ ] BASIL HUME: A PORTRAIT Tony Castle (ed.) £3.50
- [ ] TERRY WAITE: MAN WITH A MISSION
      Trevor Barnes £2.95
- [ ] PRAYING THROUGH PARADOX Charles Elliott £2.50
- [ ] TIMELESS AT HEART C. S. Lewis £2.50
- [ ] THE POLITICS OF PARADISE Frank Field £3.50
- [ ] THE WOUNDED CITY Trevor Barnes £2.50
- [ ] THE SACRAMENT OF THE WORD Donald Coggan £2.95
- [ ] IS THERE ANYONE THERE? Richard MacKenna £1.95

All Fount paperbacks are available through your bookshop or newsagent, or they can be ordered by post from Fount Paperbacks, Cash Sales Department, G.P.O. Box 29, Douglas, Isle of Man. Please send purchase price plus 22p per book, maximum postage £3. Customers outside the UK send purchase price, plus 22p per book. Cheque, postal order or money order. No currency.

NAME (Block letters) ⸻⸻⸻⸻

ADDRESS ⸻⸻⸻⸻⸻

⸻⸻⸻⸻⸻⸻

⸻⸻⸻⸻⸻⸻